Oct 2001

GLEANINGS

ESSAYS ON EXPANSIVE LANGUAGE with
PRAYERS FOR VARIOUS OCCASIONS

GLEANINGS

ESSAYS ON EXPANSIVE LANGUAGE *with* PRAYERS FOR VARIOUS OCCASIONS

Edited by

RUTH A. MEYERS • PHOEBE PETTINGELL

 CHURCH

CHURCH PUBLISHING INCORPORATED, NEW YORK

Library of Congress Cataloging-in-Publication Data

Gleanings : essays on expansive language with prayers for various occasions/
edited by Ruth A. Meyers and Phoebe Pettingell.
      p. cm.
  ISBN 0-89869-334-9 (pbk.)
   1. Episcopal Church—Liturgy. 2. Liturgical language—English. 3.
Church year—Prayer-books and devotions—English. 4. Episcopal
Church—Prayer-books and devotions—English.   I. Meyers, Ruth A.,
1957- . II. Pettingell, Phoebe.
  BX5940 .G54 2001
  264'.03—dc21
                        00-069372

Church Publishing Incorporated
445 Fifth Avenue
New York NY 10016

www.churchpublishing.org

5 4 3 2 1

CONTENTS

Pastoral Needs

Pastoral Offices

Other Prayers

Prayers from the Mothers of the Church

ACKNOWLEDGMENTS

An Advent Bidding and An Advent Litany were written by Bruce Jenneker, Associate Rector, Trinity Church, Boston, Massachusetts, for use at Washington National Cathedral, and are included here with his permission.

The All Saints' Day Litany of Saints was written by Elizabeth Morris Downie, Rector of St. Jude's Episcopal Church, Fenton, Michigan, for a quiet day. It was previously published in the newsletter of the Association of Diocesan Liturgy and Music Commissions and is included here with her permission.

The Litany of Remembrance, written for the tenth-anniversary celebration of the Council for Women's Ministries of the Episcopal Church, is also published in *Women's Uncommon Prayers: Our Lives Revealed, Nurtured, Celebrated* edited by Elizabeth Rankin Geitz, Marjorie A. Burke, and Ann Smith (Harrisburg, PA: Morehouse Publishing, 2000) and is used here with permission.

The Eucharistic Prayer from the writings of Julian of Norwich was adapted by Paula S.D. Barker, Associate Professor of Historical Theology, and Leonel L. Mitchell, Professor Emeritus, Seabury-Western Theological Seminary, Evanston, Illinois, using Eucharistic Prayer Form B in *Enriching Our Worship 1*. It is included here with their permission.

INTRODUCTION

IN 1994 THE 71ST GENERAL CONVENTION directed the Standing Liturgical Commission to continue to develop supplemental expansive-language liturgical texts. Leadership for this work was assigned to Phoebe Pettingell, newly appointed to the commission from the Diocese of Fond du Lac. Turning to those with whom she had served on the Prayer Book and Liturgy Committee at the 1994 Convention, she gathered a committee: Sister Jean Campbell, OSH, a member of the Order of St. Helena in Vails Gate, New York; the Rev. Gregory Howe, then Rector of Christ Church, Dover, Delaware; the Rev. Jennifer M. Phillips, then Rector of St. John the Evangelist, Boston, Massachusetts; and myself, the Rev. Ruth A. Meyers, then Diocesan Liturgist in the Diocese of Western Michigan.

This committee has now worked together through two triennia (and several job changes and moves by members of the committee!). Our work has included the preparation of a substantial body of new material for the Eucharist and Daily Offices, approved by the 1997 General Convention and published in *Enriching Our Worship 1*, and the development of expansive-language materials for "Ministry with the Sick or Dying" and "Burial of a Child," approved by the 2000 General Convention for publication as *Enriching Our Worship 2*.

Our work has built upon the work of previous committees, who not only developed texts but also formulated principles undergirding their work. This continuing story is traced in brief here at the beginning of my essay, "Treasures New and Old: Imagery for Liturgical Prayer." The underlying principles were discussed and elaborated more fully at a 1993 theological consultation on language and liturgy sponsored by the Standing Liturgical Commission.*

But all of us current members of the Expansive Language Committee have also brought our particular experiences, including significant pastoral experience in different contexts, and our

---

* For papers and a summary of the discussions, see Ruth A. Meyers, ed., *How Shall We Pray? Expanding Our Language about God*, Liturgical Studies Two (New York: Church Hymnal Corporation, 1994).

own studies, all of which have shaped our approach to this work of crafting expansive-language liturgical texts. Over the years, our meetings have included conversations on such subjects as the qualities of liturgical prayer; the importance of prayer in a truly American vernacular; and theological principles for the use of expansive language. Usually these conversations have taken place in the context of writing and editing specific texts.

The essays in this volume have given some of us the opportunity to reflect in a more focused way on this work we have been doing. Jennifer Phillips proposes that good liturgy must be, among other things, virtuous, musical, evocative, hospitable, and just. Phoebe Pettingell addresses some of the issues involving common prayer in a church where, for the vast majority of English speakers, the vernacular is American English. In my own essay, I discuss some of the theological foundations for the use of expansive liturgical language. Gregory Howe ponders the process of Prayer Book revision in the past and the potential impact of new technology on the next revision of The Book of Common Prayer. We hope that these essays offer the church a fuller understanding of our intentions and our principles in the task entrusted to us.

In the labor of proposing liturgical texts, much is brought to the table, but only a fraction of it appears in materials presented to General Convention for approved use in the Episcopal Church. Some materials are "occasional": that is, produced for such specific occasions as the feast of a saint; mourning for those killed in random violence (see "A Pilgrimage of Prayer for Healing the Body of Christ"); or celebration of a transition in the life of an individual or a congregation. To date, the focus of approved expansive language materials, overseen by the Standing Commission on Liturgy and Music (SCLM) and passed by the General Convention, has been prayers for general occasions: Morning and Evening Prayer, the Holy Eucharist, services of healing, the burial of a child. Our "gleanings" consist of prayers written for specific events: feasts and fasts of the Church year and the calendar of saints; pastoral occasions, needs and offices; celebration of specific events; and a series of "Prayers from the Mothers of the Church"—that form a parallel to the prayers of Church "Fathers" like St. Chrysostom and St. Francis which already appear in The Book of Common Prayer.

The members of the Expansive Language Committee are indebted to the Standing Commission on Liturgy and Music, as a body and individually, for their support of our work. Presiding Bishop Frank Griswold, who chaired the Standing Liturgical Commission from 1991–1997, urged us to publish our gleanings, and we are grateful for his encouragement. Frank Tedeschi, at Church Publishing Incorporated, helped nurture this project as it evolved into a collection of essays as well as prayers. The texts in Part II were typed in a standard electronic format by Cynthia Hallas, at the time a student from the Diocese of Central Pennsylvania in the Master of Divinity program at Seabury-Western Theological Seminary, and I am grateful for her assistance in this work.

We hope that these essays and prayers give you a deeper understanding of liturgical prayer and expansive language, and that they are a contribution to the Episcopal Church's continuing work of discerning the voice of our common prayer.

Ruth A. Meyers
Feast of Mary and Martha of Bethany, 2000

I.
ESSAYS ON
EXPANSIVE LANGUAGE

PRAYING RIGHTLY
The Poetics of Liturgy

JENNIFER M. PHILLIPS

GOOD LITURGY MUST BE VIRTUOUS. We seldom think of worship in that term, which has been thought of historically as the perfecting of the powers of the soul: maturing its reason, memory, will, desire, and intuition; and motivating and training the person to do good. We know that worship aims to praise and honor and thank God. We know that our voices and intentions join in it with the chorus of the heavenly hosts singing "Holy, Holy, Holy." But our worship also shapes and changes us. God and human beings conspire—breathe together—in this process of formation. Worship is moral formation, and not merely by means of its content, but by its qualities as well.

I want to focus on several key qualities of liturgical texts and the moral dimension of these. I will offer nine principles for good liturgical texts, not claiming these to be exhaustive but simply to be essential to virtuous worship. They are not ranked in any order, but are meant to intertwine.

TEXTS MUST BE MUSICAL. As a poet, I like to start here! Good liturgy (and preaching) is shamelessly seductive on behalf of God. It woos the heart of all present for the Bridegroom. It stirs desire and joy.

The sound of the texts must move and bring delight, invite attention. Among the five senses, hearing is arguably first for most participants in stirring them toward goodness. We hear the Word—not just its content but the sound of it in our ear. The particularity of that sound evokes emotion and memory, whether it is said or sung.

Language has distinctive rhythms particular to occasion, to geography and culture. Local liturgical practice should allow the music of the neighborhood to find a voice in it. The preacher brings her or his language rhythms to the texts, as do lectors, deacons, presiders, intercessors, and the people as they respond and sing. The sounds of the building and the street blend with the texts and with the silences in a particular poetry.

Generally, though, a majority of liturgical texts must also express the music of language in the larger culture. The music of language, like any music, may be appreciated across time and space by those with an educated ear. The music of language does change in time and place. Our ears detect the differences of urban or rural pacing, northern or southern accent, nineteenth- or twentieth-century vocabulary and phrasing. To honor the activity of God among the current assembly in the present moment, that music of language must resonate to its own time and place and not sound foreign.

For example, every Anglican recognizes the measured, stately cadences of the King's English circa 1600. Nowhere is this more beautifully epitomized than Bishop Reynolds's General Thanksgiving:

> we thine unworthy servants do give thee most humble and
> hearty thanks for all thy goodness and loving-kindness to us,
> and to all men. We bless thee for our creation, preservation,
> and all the blessings of this life.[1]

The long lines and parallel phrases fall gracefully and slowly, defying anyone who would rush through their praying. This is not simple iambic pentameter, however; there is a dance rhythm to it, with trochees and anapests adding their tripping unaccented syllables.

The eucharistic prayer of this same period is, perhaps, less eloquent (note, for example, the multiple clauses and inordinate length of the sentence), but it carries a similar music:

> Wherefore, O Lord and heavenly Father, according to the
> institution of thy dearly beloved Son, our Savior Jesus Christ,
> we thy humble servants do celebrate, and make here before

> thy divine Majesty, with these thy holy gifts, the memorial
> which thy Son hath willed us to make, having in remembrance
> his blessed passion, mighty resurrection, and glorious ascen-
> sion, rendering unto thee most hearty thanks, for the innu-
> merable benefits procured unto us by the same, entirely desir-
> ing thy fatherly goodness, mercifully to accept this our Sacri-
> fice of praise and thanksgiving: most humbly beseeching thee
> to grant, that by the merits and death of thy Son Jesus Christ,
> and through faith in his blood, we and all thy whole church,
> may obtain remission of our sins, and all other benefits of his
> passion.[2]

To most American ears, especially young ones, the music of this text is cumbersome and convoluted. The sense gets lost between the commas and semicolons. What was in its day a common (if educated) speech, becomes to later ears courtly, and strange, and very English. Some will argue that the historical feel of this language evokes for them the transcendence, kingliness, and otherness of God. Others find it soporific and alienating. In 1936, soon-to-be-bishop Stephen Bayne said of the 1928 Prayer Book General Confession, "I wish I didn't have to ask my people to make this liturgical confession in such high-falutin' language, because I know that the chances of their getting beyond a profound admiration for Elizabethan syntax are very slim indeed."[3] No one could argue that the language of these texts is a vernacular for the American church, a language understood and used by ordinary people here. Yet Anglican liturgical language was always intended to be in the vernacular of those who prayed it, as we read in the preface to the first Book of Common Prayer, by the first architects of Anglican liturgy.[4]

The music of American language is, by comparison to the language of England in the 1600s, brisk and declarative, touched by jazz rhythms and a sense of space and energy. Consider this collect, one of the few entirely new to the 1979 Prayer Book, written by Massey Shepherd for the Fifth Sunday after the Epiphany:

> Set us free, O God, from the bondage of our sins, and give us
> the liberty of that abundant life which you have made known
> to us in your Son our Savior Jesus Christ.

Compare the language of the third eucharistic prayer of the English *Alternative Service Book* of 1980 to the first eucharistic prayer of the American *Enriching Our Worship 1*:

> Send the Holy Spirit on your people
> and gather into one in your kingdom
> all who share this one bread and one cup,
> so that we, in the company of all the saints,
> may praise and glorify you for ever,
> through him from whom all good things come,
> Jesus Christ our Lord. (English)

> Grant that we who share these gifts
> may be filled with the Holy Spirit
> and live as Christ's Body in the world.
> Bring us into the everlasting heritage
> of your daughters and sons,
> that with [_____and] all your saints,
> past, present, and yet to come,
> we may praise your Name for ever. (American)

While the difference is subtle, the American phrases typically have a more irregular rhythm and seem to lean forward by means of their unaccented syllables.

Consider the prayer, "For Rest," proposed to General Convention 2000 and subsequently included in *Enriching Our Worship 2*:

> O God my refuge and strength: in this place of unrelenting
> light and noise, enfold me in your holy darkness and silence,
> that I may rest secure under the shadow of your wings.

Effective liturgical texts must be comfortably sayable and singable, with a music that pleases the ear (or at least most ears). Compared to the elaborately spiraling phrases of Reformation English, or the measured tread of modern English liturgy, contemporary American poetic prose likes to stride, even gallop, forward to the point, with only that elaboration and repetition which serves its plain meaning.

Good liturgical language is evocative. Having just made a claim for American dynamic plain speaking, I believe that it is also vital that liturgical texts be *thick*, that is, layered with allusion and meaning. This is where history is drawn in, along with Scripture. The choice of vocabulary and imagery must be rich enough to interest the mind and traditional enough to activate the memory of the community and the individual, bringing out from the liturgical storehouse that which is old and that which is new, and finding them to be organically connected, not separate things.

The prayer just cited draws its reference to God as refuge and strength from the psalms, and its expansive, mythological image of protecting wings from the versicle for Compline from the night office of the fourth century, which is itself drawn from Psalm 17. The unrelenting light and noise is the environment of our own twentieth-century hospital (or urban neighborhood). The holy darkness recalls the apophatic tradition of the medieval contemplatives and Dylan Thomas's "close and holy darkness," not to mention the universal experience of the womb.

When the 1979 Prayer Book was published, many found the modernity of its language striking, and some accused it of having abandoned tradition. One has only to take Marion J. Hatchett's detailed *Commentary on the American Prayer Book*[5] in hand to discover that the vast majority of fresh-sounding prayers drew phrases from many layers of Christian tradition: Sarum rite, Cranmer, previous prayer books, and books from other parts of the Anglican Communion. There are also borrowings from Gelasian, Veronese, Gregorian, Benedictine, Old Roman, Eastern Orthodox (including patristic), and other ancient sources, plus the Anglican divines. Most allude to or quote Scripture. As with the newest texts approved by General Convention in the year 2000, tradition is by no means abandoned. It is thickly layered in.

EFFECTIVE LITURGICAL IMAGERY NEEDS VIGOR. It should be inspiring, thus stirring the will to pray and to act well; that ancient cardinal virtue—fortitude—finds its expression here. Such liturgy fosters strength of soul and helps overcome fear. Practicing the same virtue it seeks to teach, the text should take some risks and offer fresh, even startling imagery, or fold in imagery that may be traditional but has been overlooked or forgotten. In this category, for example, is the evocative expansive-language eucharistic prayer of 1997, with creation imagery drawn from the book of Job—"the morning stars sing your praises" (Job 38:7); "[you] enclosed the sea when it burst out from the womb" (Job 38:8)—and a description of Jesus who gave "himself for us, a fragrant offering" (Ephesians 5:2). The language of prayer needs juiciness and passion, as generations of contemplative Christians have taught us.

GOOD LITURGICAL IMAGERY SHOULD FALL BETWEEN THE EXTREMES. Although we don't want worship imagery that "plays it safe," neither do we want it to go too far afield, becoming either quaint or banal, arcane or trite. To find the mean between the fresh and boring is a delicate discernment. For example, the image from Matthew 23:37 of the hen with her young is touching in the Gospel context, but when it was introduced into a eucharistic prayer for evaluation in 1987, a majority of Episcopalians found it jarring, even silly. Eucharistic Prayer C took risks in conjuring "the vast expanse of interstellar space" (one of the most satisfying modern phrases to roll on the tongue as a presider, in my experience) and "this fragile earth, our island home." Howard Galley must have had in his mind's eye as he drafted this prayer the view of the earth from space, quite new at that time. "Island earth" became a little hackneyed by the 1980s, but as time goes by it may emerge again as fresh and compelling, and touching our environmental conscience in a powerful way. The most striking images of liturgical prayer often need a few years of "wearing in" before they begin to feel homey instead of strange.

Effective liturgical language is just. The virtue of justice renders each its due. Justice first looks to the Creator whose justice is perfect and then to all fellow-creatures, each with its proper dignity as it is created by and images God. Liturgy enacts justice when it is truthful and when it seeks commonweal. Since it will fall short inevitably of perfect truth, it must also be humble. Thus in the choice of the content of our prayers and also in the words we select, our liturgical texts must be mindful of the injuries we may do one another through our prejudices of class and gender and other human difference. By word and mode of speaking we must seek to lift up those cast down, heal those suffering and broken, cry out for those oppressed and abandoned, comfort those who mourn, and remind ourselves of our created connection to all people and to the natural world.

Beauty furthers justice, and justice is beautiful. In the two, we glimpse the right ordering of the creation by its Author. The parts are all related to each other in a proper discipline and mutuality and obedience. Art, by its beauty, communicates the truth of the artist, and of what the artist sees and conveys, to the observer, with the intent that the observer be moved, enter into empathy, experience compassion. A Bach chorale, even to a listener who may not understand a word of the German text, lifts the soul (or at least, most souls) toward transcendence and unfolds a vision of humankind and the world as cohesive, meaningful, joyful, poignant. A lovely eucharistic prayer conveys themes of the story of God's saving love in history, moves those praying to gratitude, offers images that bring delight and others that stir compunction, repentance, and hope. Our liturgical texts people our imaginations with the lovely faces of the saints. They lead us beside waters, both still and rolling like thunder, and across green pastures, and down city streets. They connect us to people of the past and those to come, and to the person of Jesus, prompting us to do good, to bear suffering, to render our thanks and praise.

LITURGICAL TEXTS MUST BE HOSPITABLE. They need to be spacious enough to allow worshipers with many sorts of experience to enter in and find a place. This is one of the reasons silence is so important as a part of texts and between texts. Silence is roomy for the thoughts and feelings and prayers of all. Here, the cardinal virtue of temperance comes to the fore, asking of every creature a measure of self-control and moderation. Temperance is taking only your fair share of creation's goods and leaving just shares for the rest of the creatures to enjoy. Temperance is founded on humble discernment of what one's share should be, given how much there is to go around among many on earth.

Liturgical prayer becomes intemperate when, for example, in an *ad hoc* pastoral prayer, the one praying attributes thoughts and feelings to those on whose behalf prayer is being voiced: "we come to you today, O God, with excitement and pleasure about the results of yesterday's presidential election." In Anglican prayer, there is a certain reserve about claiming to express the feelings of others. The authors of effective texts try hard to put themselves in the shoes of a diversity of people and congregations so as to be hospitable to difference of experience. In a prayer for healing, they ask: what would this feel like to the person in the room who asked for years to be healed of disease and never was, or whose mother just died, or the person who is so bowed down with trouble as to feel abandoned by God? Is there room for each of these people as this prayer is spoken?

LITURGICAL TEXTS NEED TO EXPRESS FITTING THEOLOGY. The compendium of our authorized liturgical materials expresses many theological viewpoints, not one, and their emphases shift over time even though there is also much continuity in the central Gospel story and the ideas about God we derive from our Scripture and traditions. No one prayer should be expected to, or can, carry the weight of conveying the "whole" story. While, for example, every eucharistic prayer ought to speak in some way of Jesus' death on the cross to deliver us from sin, not every one need use the word "sacrifice," or "propitiation," to do so. Some prayers may emphasize

creation as tarnished by sin, while others stress its original goodness and the ways God may still be detected at work in its loveli-
ness. All our theological language is approximate, is metaphorical,
and must be offered humbly. We do not define God by our words.
Theological language is poetic. It alludes to God's qualities as best
we can understand and imagine them. It leans toward God.
Through our language we glimpse God as through a lattice, with
some truth, but not fully or perfectly.

Theological aptness requires the exercise of the virtue of pru-
dence, that is, right reasoning grounded in our practical sense.
Augustine described this virtue, saying that one who would "love
wisely discerns the means leading to the Beloved amid obstacles
which would bar the way." Our texts may constitute a means
toward the beloved or may raise some of those obstacles on the
way. Because of our diversity of human experience, one person's
means is another's obstacle. Therefore, a plurality of texts is helpful in allowing a variety of people to move toward the Beloved in
prayer. Negotiation and kindness, forbearance, even humor, helps
in community as we try to accommodate our conflicting individual and congregational tastes and ideas, "seeking to keep the
happy mean between too much stiffness in refusing, and too much
easiness in admitting variations."[6]

The majority of imagery used to convey theology is biblical.
This is as true of contemporary texts as it was of the materials
from past centuries. As the Anglican Communion has grown into
a global community, and each province within it becomes increasingly multicultural and cosmopolitan, old scriptural sources are
mined for evocative and fresh insights about God and humanity.
Recent texts in *Enriching Our Worship 1* and *Enriching Our Worship 2* have made use of the creation imagery from Job 38 and the
depiction of holy Wisdom from Proverbs and the apocryphal book
of Sirach (Ecclesiasticus), for example. New collects incorporate
such biblical images as God as "shield and armor of light"
(Romans 13:12); Jesus as a "fragrant offering" (Ephesians 5:2);
God as the one who "spread the sky like a tent" (Psalms 104:2;
Isaiah 40:22); and the Eucharist as "the bread of angels" (Psalms
78:25). New texts tend to use, naturally enough, contemporary
translations of the Bible, so that those who pray can hear ancient
wisdom in a fresh, accessible way.

LITURGICAL TEXTS SHOULD BE ELEGANT. For scientists, an elegant theory or proof is one which is simple and economical, comprehensive, and truly descriptive. Elegance in liturgical texts means that they have enough words to convey what is intended, without excess. They describe reality as truly as we can manage to do it. They are dignified and accessible. They aim to unify those praying in shared purpose. They cover the ground, theologically, when the many texts are taken together. They point towards God and God's incarnation and Spirit.

ULTIMATELY, THOSE LITURGICAL TEXTS that will survive over decades, generations, and occasionally centuries of use are those which touch the hearts and minds of many congregations across differences of place and time, bringing together something universal and something particular, something old and something new. Successful texts are those which are cherished. In times of stress and distress, they contain the phrases which spring to the lips for comfort and strength. In times of joy, their words leap to mind as fitting praise for the God who is good beyond all our describing.

NOTES

[1] BCP 1662; spellings have been modernized and regularized.

[2] BCP 1549; spellings have been modernized and regularized.

[3] John Booty, *An American Apostle: The Life of Stephen Fielding Bayne, Jr.* (Valley Forge PA: Trinity Press International, 1997).

[4] See BCP 1979, pp. 866–67.

[5] New York: Seabury, 1981.

[6] Preface, BCP 1979, p. 9.

"I Hear America Praying"

Liturgy, the American Vernacular, and Expansive Language

PHOEBE PETTINGELL

LET ME BEGIN WITH A STORY about a young woman growing up in the 1950s and '60s. She is an Episcopalian living in a community in the Midwest of the United States. In church, she hears the sonorous Tudor cadences of The Book of Common Prayer, with readings from the King James Bible. In school, she participates in dramatic readings from Shakespeare plays, encountering much the same language. She studies a great deal of later British literature, as well, and models her writing style on it. American literature, which she occasionally studies, always seems to be about regionalism: the New England of Hawthorne and Frost, Huck Finn's Middle America, Faulkner's South, Steinbeck's West—places where people "talk funny." In her community, people are conscious of speaking "English teacher's standard"—a language as free from regional dialect or accent as possible. When these people travel, nobody places them as being from any particular part of this country; possibly not even *from* this country. Living on the edge of a major city, she and her fellow-citizens identify themselves as cosmopolitans—not of that great Midwest metropolis, but as people who feel at home in New York, San Francisco, or London.

They do not quite speak of England as "home," the way certain colonials in Australia, Africa, or Canada once did (people who had actually been born in Melbourne, Cape Town, or Toronto, and never set foot in the British Isles), but these Americans are not so different in their refusal to claim the culture in which they live. Very likely, the English humor magazine, *Punch*, lies on their coffee tables. Their children tend to be "sent east" to college. The young woman, whose story this is, thinks of herself—she has been encouraged to do so—as an Easterner, or perhaps, at heart, English. After all, she is an Anglican (a word she is taught at church to prefer to "Episcopalian"). Along with the bland, radio announcer accent, she has picked up at school a number of phrases from British slang, certain English locutions, even a few British spellings of words.

When this young woman gets to her East Coast college, for the first time she encounters working, living American writers—men and women whose speech and prose show the hallmarks of various specific regions. They demonstrate that style consists not of aping the customs of an admired culture, but comes through recognizing and accepting the locutions of one's own environment. This is a hard lesson. The young woman must re-tune her ear to learn to use the once-despised inflections and idioms of the American vernacular. But while she is training herself to absorb native speech patterns, her rather belated, close study of American literature reveals that her own experience has actually followed the pattern of English-speaking cultures as they spread from their mother country across oceans. What F.O. Matthiessen called "the American Renaissance" came about when writers like Emerson, Melville, Dickinson, and Thoreau renounced the British literary models they had been taught, to develop forms of writing based on the American cadences they heard from their neighbors and families.

This young woman's voyage of discovery—which is partly my own—can also be taken as a parable illustrating the crossroads at which the Episcopal Church finds itself in its current liturgies. Reformers who worked on the 1979 Prayer Book certainly understood the necessity—to use the often-cited words of Article XXIV—of creating common prayer "in a tongue . . . understanded of the people."[1] In making the transition, however, from a Tudor (or, in some cases, bastard-Tudor) liturgical language to rites for the twentieth century, there was an understandable tendency to stick with the "literary" (i.e., British) style which people who had grown up on the 1928 Prayer Book, along with the Authorized Version and/or Revised Standard Version of the Bible, naturally associated with Anglican prayer.

Of course, our prayer books made a few concessions to the differences between the American and British vernacular almost from the beginning of the Episcopal Church. Americans saying Morning Prayer confession were not required to recite, "Spare thou *them*, O God, who confess their faults . . ."; we substituted *those*. Nor did the Episcopal Church persist with "Our Father *which* art in heaven," the English spelling of *shew* for *show* in the *Venite*, or "Ye *that* do truly and earnestly repent you of your sins." These particular Britishisms would have sounded quaint even to Anglicans in the United States—a people more attuned than the general population to the sound of our common language as spoken in England.

Nevertheless, the vernacular of the Prayer Book—throughout the 1979 book—remains more British than we consciously realize. Over time, the locutions which make it so have become subtle and unobtrusive. We rarely think of them as being un-American at all. To the outsider, though, or to the ear sensitive to nuances of usage, they sound, if not "English," then slightly stilted. Would American speech opt for the phrase, "heirs of your eternal kingdom"? Yes, a biblical concept is referred to here, but the very choice of this way of expressing it sounds "Old World." Many Americans—I include myself—continue a love affair with British language: consider the widespread success of *Masterpiece Theater* and Merchant/Ivory movies. A significant percentage of the members of this church take pride in their Anglo-Saxon or Celtic forebears in the same way Lutherans, say, hold on to customs brought from Germany, Scandinavia, or the Baltic nations. At the same time, though, as we hear more and more liturgies written in contemporary language, we must acknowledge that, whatever our ethnic backgrounds, we actually *think* mostly in American rhythms and idioms. Prayers which claim to be contemporary and grounded in a particular culture, yet ignore that culture's language patterns, risk sounding mannered, inauthentic.

The development of "expansive language" liturgies came about as many Episcopalians realized that the voice of women had been largely excluded from the language of contemporary liturgical prayer (a realization which, contrary to the propaganda of detractors, went beyond objections to the use of the masculine to represent the generic). By the 1980s, people were reading the prayers of women mystics—Teresa of Ávila in the sixteenth century and Thérèse of Lisieux in the nineteenth, Hildegard of Bingen in the twelfth, and Julian of Norwich in the fifteenth. It began to dawn on our consciousness that there are characteristics of women's prayer different from the way men express themselves in speaking to God. It does not matter here whether those differences spring from culture or nature: they exist. And this voice—often ecstatic, frequently lamenting, by turns gentle or angry—was absent from our corporate liturgies, and rarely present even in Anglican anthologies of prayers for private devotions. One of the initiatives of expansive language has been to bring prayers and canticles by these women and some of their sisters in religion into the liturgy (such as the prayers from the mothers of the church, which appear in *Enriching Our Worship 1*, *Enriching Our Worship 2*, and also in this volume).

Yet, in confronting the problems of developing a language that would allow woman's voice a place in corporate worship, those charged with the task kept running up against linguistic issues. These had less to do with gender alone than with the gulf between the language still considered suitable for Anglican prayer in Episcopal churches, and the way Americans habitually express themselves in speech and writing—even the most elevated kind of writing. When what is now Eucharistic Prayer C first appeared in the early 1970s, it seemed natural enough to us that it should be laced with echoes of English poets, John Donne and T.S. Eliot in particular. What then seemed contemporary were its evocative allusions to outer space, a new frontier humans were beginning to explore. A decade or so later, some of us began to wonder just why all its references should come from English poets, instead of American ones. A prayer deriving phrases from Phillips Brooks, after all, could have proved equally effective. No, it was not simply that the voices of women were absent from our rites: the authentic voices of our culture were muted. Indeed, many of the problems with our language of prayer have turned out on closer examination to be, not gender-related, but cultural—problems common to all Americans.

An outstanding example—in this case, one common to most Christian churches in the United States—comes with the use of the word "Lord" in respect to Jesus. In most of the familiar English translations of Scripture, *Kyrie*—a form of address indicating the speaker may be addressing a person of superior social status—is translated *Lord*. This doesn't create confusion for a British listener, who knows that even judges and retired Anglican bishops should be called "M'Lud." For the American hearer, however, *Lord* is primarily associated with the Old Testament translation of *Adonai*, on one hand, and with fairy tales, on the other. Thus, when directed to Jesus, "Lord" is heard as messianic proclamation, even when the person addressing him merely means something like "Sir" (the New Revised Standard Version in fact translates it this way, when appropriate). In this sense, *Lord* helps render the Gospel story perilously close to "Once upon a time," for some listeners. For a different group, proclamation of Jesus' godhead appears so indisputable that they cannot understand why everybody didn't instantly follow him. Some of the problems inherent in these misreadings spill over into our prayers where the word "Lord" often ends up sounding synonymous with "Almighty"—further confusing its association with both the first and second persons of the Trinity.

In a variety of ways, American vernacular proves to be one of those issues of inculturation our liturgies have yet to fully engage. Anscar J. Chupungco, OSB, insists that the use of prayer language rising out of a particular ethos is essential to a vital church:

> Liturgical inculturation is basically the assimilation by the liturgy of local cultural patterns. It means that liturgy and culture share the same pattern of thinking, speaking, and expressing themselves through rites, symbols, and artistic forms. In short, the liturgy is inserted into the culture, history and tradition of the people among whom the Church dwells. It begins to think, speak, and ritualize according to the local cultural pattern. If we settle for anything less than this, the liturgy of the local Church will remain at the periphery of our peoples' cultural experience.[2]

The justly admired *A New Zealand Prayer Book* has adopted the vernacular of its own country. What you hear in its phrases is clearly liturgical language, rather than what is heard on the streets of Auckland or Christchurch. Nevertheless, we get an authentic linguistic expression of a particular place which has discovered how to be "Anglican" in its own mode. But, for the same reason, when used in chapels and churches in the United States, *A New Zealand Prayer Book* strikes the ear as an exotic transplant. If we are to consider it a model, we must follow its example, not by incorporating Maori imagery and cadences into our worship as "poetic" expansions, but by recognizing—by analogy—that we, too, have American elements which have yet to make it into the liturgies of the Episcopal Church.

To cite only one of many possible instances, contemporary hymnals show more and more evidence of the significant part African-American culture has played in shaping ours. Recent linguistic research has traced the enormous influence of "Black English" on general speech. In 1970, Ralph Ellison wrote, "There is a *de'z* and *do'z* of slave speech sounding beneath our most polished Harvard accents, and if there is such a thing as a Yale accent, there is a Negro wail in it, doubtless introduced there by Old Yalie John C. Calhoun, who probably got it from his mammy." The novelist is speaking here about accent, but his own writings explore the way rhythms and locutions percolate through a culture, freshening tired phrases with lively idioms and engaging cadences. In the same way, Amerindian culture plays a significant role in many regions; its pacing and turns of phrase also affect the way all other peoples in such an area express themselves. And increasingly, American language is shaped by Spanish. It is doubtful that a sensitive ear could read a page written by an American novelist or poet and confuse the idiom with that of an English-speaking person of another part of the world. Should not these elements be incorporated into the flow of our prayer? Are they not intrinsic to the language in which we think and express ourselves, the very core of what makes us who we are?

Anglican liturgy has traditionally been based on Scripture. However, what is evoked by scriptural imagery alters in different times and places, since eras and communities resonate to different metaphors. The aspects of the salvation story we concentrate on serve both as evangelistic tools for bringing the Gospel to those who have not grasped it and as expressions of the way we understand ourselves. In Christmas carols, for example, the same familiar images attendant on the humble birth of the Godhead in human form—the proletarian shepherds; the homage of the wise men from the East with their royal gifts; the mother's care for her child; angels singing "hosanna in the highest"; even the stable animals themselves (derived from medieval apocryphal gospels)— spotlight different aspects of the incarnation and its effect on the world, depending upon the audience being addressed.

Consider the beginnings of the eucharistic prayers we regularly use in worship. The ancient prayer of St. Basil (Eucharistic Prayer D) lingers on God's splendor and majesty and the creation of humankind, whereas Cranmer goes directly to the atonement of Christ's death on the cross for our sins. In two more modern examples, Prayer B invokes the Word throughout the history of salvation "in the calling of Israel to be your people; in your Word spoken through the prophets; and above all in the Word made flesh, Jesus, your Son." The creation of heaven and earth itself is described in Prayer C, though as previously noted, these images are derived less from Scripture itself than from poetry, obviously inspired by the first pictures of our own planet taken from space, "this fragile earth, our island home." The cosmology of Genesis perhaps conflicts too sharply with most contemporary Episcopalians' understanding of a vast universe in which earth is not the center. In addition, the heritage of "creationist" arguments against Darwinian evolution unfortunately seems to have made many Higher Protestants uncomfortable with biblical passages often used to buttress literal interpretations.

What fresh influences in the culture led to the development of expansive-language texts? A common assumption is that the movement arose out of feminism, ordination of women, and the influence of such theologians as Rosemary Radford Ruether, Elizabeth Schüssler Fiorenza, and Mary Daly. Certainly, all these played a role, but their influence has been overdetermined. Of equal, if not greater, importance to the climate that produced the post-1979 rites was the self-help movement, partly deriving from Jung's vision of a divine nurturing force that corresponded with part of the inner psyche. This consoling view—a sharp contrast to Freud's more stoic vision of an inner self fraught with competitive and self-destructive urges—helped to inspire new prayers invoking a God whose love could be compared to that of a mother for her infant.

An early attempt at an inclusive-language eucharistic prayer focused on the female emanation of God called Wisdom, from the Apocrypha. Another adapted Christ's words addressed to Jerusalem in Matthew 23:37, describing how, in his love, Jesus "yearned to draw all the world to himself, as a hen gathers her young under her wings, yet we would not." Neither of these images was deemed helpful. However, another one (now Eucharistic Prayer 1 in *Enriching Our Worship 1*), which emphasized a God of blessing and graciousness, *was*—its nurturing language striking a chord in the many who have attended Alcoholics Anonymous or similar twelve-step groups. It is worth noting that the language of this prayer probably goes further toward one kind of high middlebrow American vernacular than any other approved liturgy in the Episcopal Church. The fact that its timeliness already sounds a bit dated only underlines the difficulties of developing a rhetoric that will sound, at once, timely and timeless.

The second eucharistic prayer in *Enriching Our Worship 1* returns to the imagery of universal creation seen in the Prayer Book's Prayer C, this time stressing the role of the Holy Spirit which "moved over the deep and brought all things into being," closer to the images of Genesis than the earlier poetic effort. Prayer 3 also evokes God's act of creation "through Jesus Christ, your eternal Word, the Wisdom from on high by whom you created all things." But this time, instead of recapitulating the description in Genesis, it calls up the language of Job 38:4–11 in which God encloses the sea after "it burst out of the womb," and seeing the power of their Creator, the morning stars and heavenly beings shout with joy. Here, ecstatic rhetoric reflects another new influence—a culture in the process of reappropriating some of the mysticism of the late Middle Ages and early Renaissance—also to be perceived in the new canticles from Anselm and Julian of Norwich.

The revival of interest in medieval writing can be traced back to Evelyn Underhill, C.S. Lewis, and T.S. Eliot's appropriation of Julian's "All shall be well" in his "Little Gidding," from *Four Quartets*. However, by the late 1980s and early '90s, even small-town bookstores might easily carry small, popular editions of *The Cloud of Unknowing* or Julian's *Showings*, while tapes and CDs of Hildegard's euphonious music abounded. Changing times may once again lead our church to turn away from these influences. It must be noted, though, that they echo strains long present in other Christian traditions that play a shaping role in our country: from the Shakers to the Pentecostals, for whom a mystical relationship with God leads to ecstatic praise.

Obviously, the problem of balancing our Anglican liturgical tradition with the ethos of American vernacular and culture is not easily resolved. Liturgy is not literature, much less common speech. In the words of Philip H. Pfatteicher, while its language "must be rooted in the 'real world'. . . its flower is in another realm."[3] Prayer is always, to some degree, an ecstatic speech. However, if we are the speakers in the rite, we must own what is said. Insincere prayer language defeats its purpose.

The closest thing to the ecstatic language of prayer is poetry (though it is certainly not identical in form or function). Poets have served our Anglican liturgies well in the past. And contemporary poetry strives for a style which reflects American vernacular in a manner also familiar to Cranmer's principles of Anglican prayer—spare and descriptive, neither quaintly archaic nor flowery; not quite the language we speak, yet readily understandable as our expression if we take the trouble to speak our best. The language of our liturgical prayer must be one that does not spill into something so colloquial that unwary visitors fear they have stumbled into an insular community no outsider can be expected to comprehend. Poetry, unlike prose, can erect a compressed structure which leads hearers, through its evocative language and scriptural imagery, to bring their own individual experiences and gifts to the encounter with the text. This is a good paradigm for rites, which effect a corporate experience—being a part of Christ's body—that is simultaneous to individuals' encounters with God. In a postmodern era, the church needs to shed the last vestiges of the kind of didactic prose beloved of the Enlightenment—where worshipers are talked at, as if in a lecture hall. But after all, the quest for an American liturgy is a fairly recent enterprise—only about a quarter of a century old. "Common Prayer" requires a combination of not-so-common elements to achieve (in no particular order): vitality of language, liturgical scholarship, a living faith, a desire to evangelize, discernment both of where we have been and where we hope to go. Certainly, we need to be watchful to make sure that all these qualities, and others as well, remain in our sights.

"I hear America singing," wrote Walt Whitman in his prophetic, hopeful mode, "the varied carols I hear." Many of Whitman's contemporaries couldn't hear these carols as expressive of a nation. Instead, they saw a confused mass of immigrants representing too many diverse ethnicities, not adding up to a union but representing a disordered patchwork of conflicting values. They feared dissolution, mob rule, anarchy. Yet Whitman was more perceptive than those who thought they were living at the end of civilization. The democratic project Whitman extolled now seems a golden age when European immigrants, recently freed slaves, Native Americans, and laborers imported from the Orient all helped strengthen a country so recently torn by civil warfare. Today, some Episcopalians are equally fearful of the new variety in our forms of worship. They worry that their church is abandoning its heritage and that we may be losing the very qualities that once unified Anglicans. In a sermon preached as part of a celebration of the 450th anniversary of The Book of Common Prayer, the Rev. Leonel Mitchell answered this with his characteristically wise liturgical understanding:

> We do Cranmer and his work no honor by gilding it and putting it on display. We best follow the lead of the first Book of Common Prayer by making liturgy live in our own day, for our own people. It is not an heirloom of our cultural heritage to be displayed in a showcase for our children to admire, it is a working tool to be used by us and them. And so today we give thanks for the gift of the English liturgy, and we ask that we may pray with our spirit and understanding, to make that liturgy alive today.[4]

The heritage of Anglican prayer is a nobly expressive one, and I am not suggesting that in any way we should abandon it. Rather, as time goes on, we should make it more and more ours, just as other provinces of the Anglican Communion are already doing. This requires us to consider deeply what actually makes our tradition of prayer. Is it Tudor language? The Episcopal Church decided not, back in the 1970s. At an even earlier date—one might say even from its origins when it opted to use the seventeenth-century Scottish form of the eucharistic prayer, rather than the English, in its first Prayer Book in 1789—the Episcopal Church concluded that it did not need to adhere slavishly to early Renaissance Protestant atonement theology. In the 1979 Prayer Book and in *Enriching Our Worship 1* and *Enriching Our Worship 2*, pre-Reformation patterns of eucharistic prayers, together with a more ancient use of the church's imagery, make their appearance. All these liturgies remain faithful to what Presiding Bishop Frank T. Griswold has called the "Trinitarian and Christological formulations which we, as Anglicans, regard as normative and the ground of our common prayer."[5]

The most frequent objection I hear to contemporary Episcopal liturgies is that they "lack the dignity" of older Book of Common Prayer rites, that today's English is an inferior medium to Cranmer's—or even to the Victorian collects that pervaded the 1928 Prayer Book and often survive intact in 1979. From a stylistic perspective, the contents of the 1928 Prayer Book in fact present a mixed bag—as indeed its predecessor did and as our current Prayer Book does. Certainly we might have avoided some of the problems inherent in the use of a contemporary vernacular, had we retained our Tudor liturgical language. We did not because— even before the trial rites leading up to the 1979 book—many of our clergy could no longer cope adequately with the rhythms and flow of its syntax, and because our young frequently complained that they did not understand it. As for arguments about the dignity and beauty of the past, even Cranmer himself—one of the world's great prose stylists—faced that very sort of opposition when he tried to supplant the Church Latin of old with his new-fangled liturgies.

The point is, once we have decided to pray in contemporary English, we must forge a contemporary language of prayer that will carry those qualities we deem necessary to corporate prayer. The Anglican reformers of the sixteenth and seventeenth centuries reshaped their own vernacular to accomplish this. We must do the same. And since we can only live in our own period, it is fruitless to regret the hand we are dealt. In every age, expressive writers make the most of the same language abused in sloppy speaking and wooden writing. Many Episcopalians argue that the American vernacular has been already appropriated by denominations who pray largely extemporaneously, whose style grates on our ears. What actually disturbs us about such prayers is not American qualities per se, but rather mannerisms which reflect another culture and tradition.

Expansive language does not represent a struggle of one neglected group against the dominant culture of our church. Rather, it represents the struggle to develop an authentic language common to all of our English-speaking worshipers in the Episcopal Church—female or male, and every ethnicity we represent—if we are to pray authentically out of our own time and place, the collective experience of who we are. On this pilgrims' way, we need to hear America praying through us and through others.

NOTES

[1] BCP 1979, p. 872.

[2] Anscar J. Chupungco, *Liturgical Inculturation* (Collegeville MN: Liturgical Press, 1992), p. 30.

[3] Philip H. Pfatteicher, *Liturgical Spirituality* (Valley Forge PA: Trinity Press International, 1997), p. xi.

[4] Leonel L. Mitchell, "The First Book of Common Prayer," *Open* (Fall 1999), p. 7.

[5] *Enriching Our Worship 1* (New York: Church Publishing Inc., 1998), p. 6.

TREASURES NEW AND OLD
Imagery for Liturgical Prayer

RUTH A. MEYERS

THE EVOLUTION OF INCLUSIVE-LANGUAGE LITURGICAL MATERIALS

IN THE EARLY 1970s, I was part of a "youth presence" at a national convention of the Girl Scouts of the USA. A key piece of legislation that year was a new version of the Girl Scout Promise, a proposal that proved to be nearly as contentious as Prayer Book revision in the Episcopal Church. What stands out in my memory is heated debate over the proposed phrase "to serve God, my country, and mankind." Some argued passionately that "mankind" was exclusive, sexist, and hence particularly unsuited for an organization devoted to girls and women. Others, arguing just as vehemently, claimed that "everyone" knew that "mankind" referred to all humanity, not just male human beings.[1]

This debate at a Girl Scout convention captures a moment in a shifting understanding and use of language in the United States. In the early 1970s, terms such as "man" and "he" were increasingly viewed as gender-specific—referring only to male human beings—rather than as generic, that is, inclusive of both females and males. Although this perception may not have been widely shared, it nonetheless affected the language of the 1979 Book of Common Prayer.

As the 1979 Prayer Book was developed, the Standing Liturgical Commission (SLC) authorized a "Committee on Sensitivity Relating to Women" to identify the concerns of women in the church and to make specific recommendations for proposed texts. This work was done mainly in committee, without great fanfare. The committee simply took draft texts and proposed more felicitous wording using inclusive language. In one of the church's official Prayer Book Studies, *Introducing the Draft Proposed Book*, Charles P. Price explained:

> In response to a widespread, though admittedly not universal, sense that the word "man" . . . can be taken to designate males only instead of including females as well, SLC has undertaken a careful review of all generic references, and has sought to eliminate ambiguity wherever possible.[2]

While many masculine nouns and pronouns were eliminated from the final drafts of the 1979 Prayer Book, generic uses of masculine language remain in some psalms (for example, Psalm 133, "how good . . . it is when brethren live together in unity"); in several citations from Scripture (for example, the opening anthems in the Rite II Burial Office and some canticles in Morning and Evening Prayer); and in most Rite I texts. According to Price, "The generic 'man' has been less systematically removed from Rite I, to preserve its traditional character better."[3]

The Committee on Sensitivity Relating to Women also expressed concern that the use of exclusively masculine names for God (Father, Son, King, Lord) evokes an image of God as male. Accordingly, the committee recommended that, insofar as possible, masculine names for God be replaced by terms denoting God's actions. Their proposal, perhaps too radical for its time, was not acted upon.

But the issue did not disappear. In 1985, the General Convention directed the Standing Liturgical Commission to "prepare inclusive language liturgies for the regular services of the church, i.e., Morning and Evening Prayer and the Holy Eucharist." Each subsequent General Convention has directed the Standing Liturgical Commission (and its successor, the Standing Commission on Liturgy and Music) to continue its work of studying, developing, and evaluating new liturgical materials.

New texts began appearing in the late 1980s. As the materials were used and evaluated, individual texts were further revised or discarded (although, unfortunately, older texts continue to be used in some places). First to appear was "Liturgical Texts for Evaluation,"[4] used and evaluated for four weeks in the fall of 1987 by a limited number of parishes as well as seminaries and two religious communities. Responses to these texts led to "Supplemental Liturgical Texts," presented to the 1988 General Convention.[5] The convention authorized experimental use of these texts after a review and revision in consultation with the House of Bishops Theology Committee. *Supplemental Liturgical Texts: Prayer Book Studies 30*[6] became available for use early in 1990. Over 800 congregations (ten percent of the parishes and missions of the Episcopal Church) were nominated by their diocesan bishop or agreed to participate in a process that included education, Sunday worship with the texts, and evaluation. Approximately half of these congregations completed this process by submitting an evaluation of their experience.

The Standing Liturgical Commission introduced a new approach in *Supplemental Liturgical Materials*,[7] authorized by the 1991 and 1994 General Conventions. Previously, the proposed materials were presented as entire liturgies, from opening acclamation through the concluding dismissal. A single pamphlet provided all the necessary texts for congregational use. In contrast, *Supplemental Liturgical Materials* was a resource book containing liturgical texts to be used in the context of a Rite II Eucharist. For example, congregations might use an opening acclamation or a eucharistic prayer from *Supplemental Liturgical Materials* while continuing to use Rite II texts for the rest of their service. This approach was intended to permit a gradual introduction to the supplemental materials and to allow congregations to purchase just one book, with texts duplicated as needed; it also required more planning and preparation than the use of a ready-made pew edition. The same approach, that is, a resource book providing texts to supplement the options available in Rite II, is taken in *Enriching Our Worship*, the collection of texts authorized by the 1997 General Convention and reauthorized by the 2000 General Convention. This book contains many of the texts found in earlier editions—although some prayers have been revised—and adds many new materials, including several canticles and a third eucharistic prayer.

The 1997 General Convention also directed the Standing Commission on Liturgy and Music to begin developing expansive-language texts for the Pastoral Offices. During the triennium which followed, a subcommittee prepared materials for Ministration with the Sick or Dying and Burial of a Child, which were approved by the 2000 Convention for publication as *Enriching Our Worship 2*.[8]

LANGUAGE AND IMAGERY: "INCLUSIVE," "BALANCED," AND "EXPANSIVE" LANGUAGE

AS DISCUSSED ABOVE, the drafters of the 1979 Prayer Book eliminated many (but not all) generic uses of masculine nouns and pronouns in the liturgies. Thus the use of gender-inclusive language to speak about humankind was not a major concern needing to be addressed in the subsequent preparation of inclusive-language worship materials. However, when the Standing Liturgical Commission began its work in 1985, they adopted a guideline requiring that language used to describe human beings be "indisputably" inclusive, a guideline it viewed as "more stringent than that used in preparing the 1979 Prayer Book."[9] For example, revisions of the canticles "The Song of Zechariah" and "The Song of Mary" refer to our "forebears" rather than "fathers," and Eucharistic Prayer 1 uses the phrase "daughters and sons." By inverting the customary sequence "sons and daughters," the text implies that neither male nor female consistently has priority. A more rigorous practice of inclusion is also apparent in the institution narrative of the supplemental eucharistic prayers, which proclaim that Jesus' blood was poured out "for you and for all," making clear that forgiveness is available to all people through Christ's sacrifice on the cross. Recognition of the diversity of human social structures is evident in the reference in Eucharistic Prayer 2 to "every tribe and language and people and nation."

The Drafting Committee also set out to reclaim the role played by women in salvation history. By referring to Abraham and Sarah, Eucharistic Prayer 1 and a new blessing make explicit the inclusion of women in the sacred story. But in the 1979 Prayer Book lectionary, many biblical stories about women are omitted or included only as optional or alternative readings, as demonstrated by Jean Campbell in a careful study of the 1979 lectionary.[10] The Episcopal Church has yet to address this deficiency, largely because our lectionary has never been considered the responsibility of those who develop supplemental worship texts. However, the Consultation on Common Texts, an ecumenical body—whose membership included a representative of the Episcopal Church—worked intentionally to add biblical stories of women when it produced the *Revised Common Lectionary*. Based on the 1979 lectionary and similar lectionaries used by other churches, the *Revised Common Lectionary* includes such stories as the women who follow Jesus and support his ministry (Luke 8:1–3), the woman healed of a hemorrhage (Mark 5:25–34), and the baptism of Lydia (Acts 16:14–15). A number of other churches, including some provinces of the Anglican Communion, have adopted the *Revised Common Lectionary*, but, in the Episcopal Church, the lectionary has been approved only for trial use.

The constant focus of the committee's energy was to deepen our language about God. As a first step, the committee defined "inclusive language" as language which more fully reflects worshipers' understanding of themselves and their experience of God as revealed in Christ. The underlying premise is that the predominant liturgical use of masculine images and language in reference to God implies that God is male, thus limiting our vision of God and making it difficult for women to see themselves as created in the image of God.

The earliest work on inclusive-language liturgical materials had two aspects. The first was the preparation of an adapted version of the Rite II forms of the Daily Offices and the Holy Eucharist. Jean Campbell has described this work as "liturgy by white-out." With the exception of the Apostles' and Nicene Creeds, the Lord's Prayer, and a few uses of "Son" in the eucharistic prayers, all masculine references to God, both nouns and pronouns, were eliminated. "Christ" and "God" were used repeatedly, and in places "Savior" or "Redeemer" replaced references to Jesus as "Lord." In the initial experimental use of these texts, worshipers reported that these changes in God-language made God seem remote and abstract. The recurrent use of "God" and "Christ" offered a very limited and impersonal image of God, and the elimination of pronouns further diminished a sense of God as personal. Accordingly, efforts to amend existing Prayer Book texts of the Eucharist were abandoned, and—at a somewhat later stage—similar adaptations of the office collects were also discarded.

Secondly, the committee composed new rites, using images from Scripture and the Christian tradition that had been under-used or absent in the liturgy of the Episcopal Church. These were not intended to replace the 1979 Prayer Book, but to deepen language about God by using a variety of prayers, each with different images of the divine, over a period of time. (This is already implicit in the 1979 Prayer Book, which includes two eucharistic prayers for Rite I and four for Rite II.) The committee described this as "balanced language":

> These texts deliberately seek a more balanced imagery in descriptions of God. . . . Care has . . . been taken to avoid an over-reliance on metaphors and attributes generally perceived as masculine, and to seek out and use images which describe God in feminine and other scripturally-based terms.[11]

More recently, the term "expansive language" has been used to emphasize the need for a wide range of language and imagery in order to speak of the inexhaustible mystery of God. Throughout the history of the project, the revisers have sought to offer a fuller vision of God by expanding the imagery used in liturgical texts.

The Episcopal Church has not been alone in seeking a fuller vision of God. Since the earliest stages, the supplemental materials have included texts prepared by the English Language Liturgical Consultation (ELLC), an ecumenical body comprising representatives of major English-speaking denominations in several countries, including the Episcopal Church. ELLC is the successor of the International Consultation on English Texts (ICET), which produced contemporary English-language translations of common liturgical texts: the Lord's Prayer, Apostles' and Nicene Creeds, *Kyrie, sursum corda, Sanctus* and *Benedictus, Agnus Dei, Gloria patri* and several canticles; these ICET texts are used in the 1979 Prayer Book. The use of inclusive language was one important guideline for the ELLC revisions of ICET texts. Accordingly, the ELLC revisions eliminate the few remaining masculine-specific references to humanity in these common texts and reduce masculine God-language. In some texts masculine pronouns are replaced by "God" or omitted altogether, while in "The Song of Mary" (*Magnificat*) and "The Song of Zechariah" (*Benedictus*) second-person pronouns ("you") replace third-person masculine pronouns ("he").[12]

FOUNDATIONS FOR EXPANSIVE GOD-LANGUAGE

TO EXPAND LITURGICAL LANGUAGE about God and God's work, the Standing Liturgical Commission explored the riches of Scripture and the Christian tradition. In biblical Hebrew and Greek the words translated "God" and "Lord" are masculine-gender nouns. But Scripture also speaks of God with a wide range of metaphorical language, using feminine as well as masculine and non-gender-specific images, and there is ample evidence in Christian tradition for the use of a multiplicity of imagery to speak about and to God.

God the Father—and Mother
Although "Father" has become a central metaphor in Christian tradition, careful study of Scripture shows that it is not the only or even the primary term used to speak about and to God. The Old Testament includes only a handful of references to God as Father. In the New Testament, "Father" is one of numerous metaphors Jesus uses to address God and teach about God. Arguments have been advanced that Jesus' use of the Aramaic *abba* is an unprecedented form of intimate address revealing Jesus' unique relationship with God, but these conclusions have been increasingly questioned by scholars. While Jesus addresses God as "Father" occasionally, the Gospels refer to God as "Father" with ever increasing frequency. Elizabeth Johnson identifies four references in Mark, fifteen in Luke, forty-nine in Matthew, and 109 in John, suggesting that the ever-increasing use of "Father" reflects theological development in the apostolic church rather than being Jesus' sole or preferred name for God. Furthermore, some scholars suggest that Jesus' use of "Father" may be intended to undercut the patriarchal authority of the Roman Empire rather than to assert a unique father-son relationship with God.[13] Elizabeth Johnson concludes, "Both the fluidity of Jesus' own language and the intent of the paternal metaphor itself in his hands allow and indeed call for other ways of Christian speaking about God in addition to the language of father."[14]

The most apparent complement to "father" is "mother." In the Old Testament, maternal imagery is one means of articulating God's compassionate love for humanity. The Hebrew word translated "compassion" or "mercy" (*rahamim*) is etymologically related to "womb" (*rehem*), suggesting an analogy between divine compassion and the intimacy and nurture of a mother's womb.

Beyond this analogy, in a few places the Old Testament explicitly tells of God giving birth (Deuteronomy 32:18; Isaiah 42:14) and portrays God as a mother who nurses her children, comforts them, and teaches them to walk (Isaiah 49:14–15, 66:12–13; Psalm 131:2; Hosea 11:1–4). Elsewhere God is described as a mother eagle (Deuteronomy 32:11–12) and as a bear robbed of her cubs (Hosea 13:8). In the New Testament, Jesus expresses a yearning to draw the world to himself by comparing himself to a mother hen who gathers her young (Matthew 23:37; Luke 13:34). Jesus' conversation with Nicodemus (John 3) uses the metaphor of birth to tell of the work of the Spirit. In the Letter of James, maternal imagery complements paternal language: "the Father of lights . . . gave us birth by the word of truth" (James 1:17–18).

Patristic and medieval writers also used maternal imagery to speak of God. Frequently "mother" emphasized the compassionate nature of God, complementing God's fatherhood. Clement of Alexandria wrote: "God Himself is love; and out of love to us became feminine. In His ineffable essence He is Father; in His compassion to us He became Mother."[15] The Cappadocian theologian Gregory of Nyssa acknowledged that both "mother" and "father" could be used in reference to God, but insisted that neither term alone was an adequate description of God:

> No one who has given thought to the way we talk about God can adequately grasp the terms pertaining to God. "Mother," for example, is mentioned [in the Song of Songs 3:11] instead of "father." Both terms mean the same, because there is neither male nor female in God. . . . Therefore every name we invent is of the same adequacy for indicating God's ineffable nature, since neither "male" nor "female" can defile the meaning of God's pure nature.[16]

Medieval writers referred not only to God as mother, but to Jesus also. Here, too, maternal imagery often indicated compassion in contrast to the awesome majesty of God. For example, the fourteenth-century mystic Julian of Norwich wrote:

> But often when our falling and our wretchedness are shown to us, we are so much afraid and so greatly ashamed of ourselves that we scarcely know where we can put ourselves. But then our courteous Mother does not wish us to fall away. . . . [Instead, we should] behave like a child. For when it is distressed and frightened, it runs quickly to its mother; and if it can do no more, it calls to the mother for help with all its might.[17]

Additionally, maternal imagery was employed by medieval writers to portray Jesus giving birth to the new creation.[18]

Our contemporary supplemental liturgical materials have both limited the use of "Father" and introduced maternal imagery. The intent has not been to eliminate liturgical use of "Father" (which remains firmly fixed in our liturgical tradition due to continuing use of the creeds and the Lord's Prayer) but rather to offer "Father" as one name among many. However, because the supplemental texts are designed to expand (though not replace) the language of the Prayer Book, "Father" was used in the early stages of the project only in the most traditional texts: the Apostles' and Nicene Creeds and the canticles "A Song of Creation" (*Benedicite*, Canticle 12) and "We Praise You, O God" (*Te Deum*, Canticle 21). Maternal imagery, based in Scripture, was introduced in a eucharistic prayer and a blessing.

Not all of the language was effective as liturgical metaphor: a statement that God "led us with cords of compassion and bands of love" (Hosea 11:4) did not provide sufficient resonance with contemporary experience (what are "cords of compassion and bands of love"?); an explicit reference to Jesus as a mother hen gathering her young (Matthew 23:37) implied for many that people are "chicks," although the prayer did not use the latter word. This prayer was revised, retaining the proclamation that God cares for us "as a mother cares for her children" but eliminating the explicit reference to Jesus as a mother hen.

With *Enriching Our Worship 1* (first approved in 1997), the principle of expansive language was deemed to be so well established in the Episcopal Church that a rigid avoidance of "Father" was considered unnecessary. Of the seventeen new canticles (which greatly expanded the church's repertoire), three were New Testament canticles that refer to God as "Father" (two of the three bless God as "Father of our Lord Jesus Christ"). But along with these canticles, "A Song of Jerusalem Our Mother" introduces maternal imagery from Isaiah (66:10–14), and three canticles include maternal language from the medieval writers Anselm of Canterbury and Julian of Norwich.

Jesus Christ, Son of God

The use of gender in reference to Jesus is more complicated. The supplemental materials, both in the liturgical texts and in commentaries on the texts, recognize that the incarnate Jesus was a male. Yet they also suggest, rather more directly than the Prayer Book, that it is not the maleness but the humanity of Jesus that is significant in the redemption of humanity. For example, the Nicene Creed proclaims that Jesus "was incarnate of the Holy Spirit and the Virgin Mary and became truly human," and Eucharistic Prayer 2 speaks of Jesus as "the holy child of God." This emphasis on Jesus' humanity rather than his masculinity accords with the oft-cited assertion of patristic writers: "what was not assumed was not redeemed."

Although the supplemental texts use masculine pronouns in acknowledgment that the incarnate Jesus was male, they do not use masculine pronouns to speak of Christ. Accordingly, the doxology in each eucharistic prayer reads, "Through Christ and with Christ and in Christ," and elsewhere the texts repeat the noun "Christ" rather than introducing a pronoun. By not using masculine pronouns, the texts imply that the divine Christ is not necessarily male, even though the incarnate Jesus was.

The texts also make very limited use of "Son." "Sending the Son" has been a classical Christian manner of expressing the redemptive activity of God in the incarnation. This language appears in one of the newer canticles (from 1 John 4:7–11) in *Enriching Our Worship 1*. But in keeping with the expansive approach to liturgical language, the eucharistic prayers speak of God's redemptive work in different ways: Eucharistic Prayer 1 prays to God, creator of the universe and giver of life, who "sent your eternal Word, made mortal flesh in Jesus"; Eucharistic Prayer 2, after describing God's work in creation, says, "you looked with favor upon Mary . . . that she might conceive and bear a son, Jesus the holy child of God"; Eucharistic Prayer 3 simply proclaims that God "gave Jesus to be human."

The Triune God

Language of "Father" and "Son" leads to questions about trinitarian language. Some claim that "Father, Son, and Holy Spirit" is the revealed name of God and must be used in order to maintain the historic identity of Christian worship.[19] But many contemporary discussions of trinitarian theology emphasize that "Father, Son, and Holy Spirit" is a shorthand way to speak of the economy of salvation. Trinitarian doctrine asserts that relationship is central to the being of God, that God is in relationship with Godself and with the world. Within God there is both unity and diversity.

Furthermore, the relations within God exist without subordination, as an equality of being.[20]

Although "Father, Son, and Holy Spirit" has been a primary way in which Christians have named the triune God, many other possibilities exist. Augustine pointed out the inadequacy of all trinitarian language: "it is not easy to find a name that will suitably express so great excellence, unless it is better to speak in this way: the Trinity, one God, of whom are all things, through whom are all things, in whom are all things."[21] In his treatise *On the Trinity* Augustine offered a number of analogies, for example, lover, beloved, and love; the mind itself, the love of it, and the knowledge of it. Julian of Norwich used images such as power, wisdom, love; source of our nature, mercy and grace.[22] Hildegard of Bingen described a brightness, a flashing forth, and a fire. In the twentieth century, Karl Rahner and Karl Barth each spoke of God as one person in three manners of subsistence, while other theologians have used the analogy of three persons in communion with one another.[23]

A glance through the section "The Holy Trinity" in *The Hymnal 1982* suggests still more images. "Holy, holy, holy" (Hymn 362) does not use a triune name but extols "God in three Persons, blessed Trinity"; "Thou, whose almighty word" (Hymn 371) calls the Trinity "wisdom, love, might" and uses an abundance of imagery to acclaim God's involvement with humanity; "Come, thou almighty King" (Hymn 365) uses "Father" and "King" but, instead of Son, speaks of the "incarnate Word" and "Savior and friend."

The supplemental texts incorporate some of this diversity of imagery into liturgical prayer. By proclaiming and invoking God who is intimately involved in creation and who gives life to the world, the texts invite Christians to enter ever more fully into the mystery of the triune God. Each of the eucharistic prayers expresses this mystery in a particular way. An alternative to the *Gloria patri* praises "the holy and undivided Trinity," and blessings use different formulations to name the triune God and speak of God's activity:

> God's Blessing be with you,
> Christ's peace be with you,
> the Spirit's outpouring be with you,
> now and always. *Amen.*

> The Wisdom of God
> the Love of God
> and the Grace of God
> strengthen you
> to be Christ's hands and heart in this world,
> in the name of the Holy Trinity. *Amen.*

In assessing these and seeking additional alternatives to the traditional "Father, Son, and Holy Spirit," we are continually challenged to find metaphors that are concrete and resonate with contemporary human experience, as well as evocative, engaging the imagination of worshipers, and drawing them deeper into the mystery of the triune God.

Lord

Gail Ramshaw pinpoints the significance of the term "Lord" in Christian tradition, including Christian liturgical prayer: "In English-language Bibles the Hebrew divine name came to be rendered LORD and Jesus came to be titled Lord. This double term LORD/Lord is shorthand for a fundamental formula of Christian faith: Jesus is titled with the name of God."[24] While some, including Ramshaw, object to using the term, because "Lord" is both a masculine term and one associated with a hierarchical social system, a strong case has been made for the continuing use of "Lord" in liturgy. The title is one of the earliest confessional names applied to Jesus as an affirmation of Christ's authority over all other powers, particularly the Roman imperial government. Furthermore, many African-American Christians have pointed out that, in their heritage, "Lord" signifies God's liberating power in contrast to the oppression of white slave masters.

Because of this ambiguity, the supplemental texts do not eliminate "Lord" altogether, but—as with other masculine titles—use alternative terms in a number of places. Where Lord clearly refers to Jesus, "Christ" or "Savior" is sometimes used. In other places "Lord" is replaced by "God." But in the creeds and in canticles and psalms, "Lord" remains where it has customarily translated an original Hebrew or Greek word, and "Lord" continues to appear in the *sursum corda* and *Sanctus* of the eucharistic prayers.

New Imagery: Divine Wisdom

Each Advent, as the familiar strains of "O come, O come, Emmanuel" echo through our worship, Episcopalians cry out, "O come, thou Wisdom from on high, who orderest all things mightily." As is true of the images in each of the six other verses, "Wisdom" is another name for the Holy One incarnate in Jesus. Yet, apart from this Advent hymn and a few other hymns, this figure has been largely absent from worship for many generations.

The biblical figure of Wisdom offers a feminine image of God. "Wisdom" is grammatically feminine in Hebrew (*hokmah*), Greek (*sophia*), and Latin (*sapientia*), and wisdom appears as a feminine persona in post-exilic writings. In the early stages of the Wisdom tradition, Wisdom, who calls people to ways of justice, truth, and righteousness (Proverbs 1:20–33, 8:1–36, 9:1–6), is portrayed as the first of God's created works and at God's side at the creation of the world (Proverbs 8:22–31). As the tradition developed, Wisdom was identified as *Torah* (Sirach 24:23; Baruch 4:1), was associated with Spirit (Wisdom of Solomon 9:17) and the divine Word (Wisdom of Solomon 9:1-2), and eventually was represented as a personification of God, one who manifests the creative and redemptive work of the divine (Wisdom of Solomon 7:22—10:21).

The Jewish Wisdom tradition was a primary resource for the early Christians who sought ways to explain their experience of Jesus and his significance in salvation history. Jesus is viewed as the messenger or child of Wisdom (e.g., Luke 7:31–35), but as Wisdom Christology develops, Jesus eventually is identified as Wisdom herself (e.g., Matthew 11:19). Descriptions of Jesus and his work echo Wisdom literature (e.g., Colossians 1:15–20—cf. Proverbs 8:22; Wisdom of Solomon 7:26; Sirach 24:9). This is particularly evident in the Gospel of John. Just as Jesus is the revealer and source of truth (John 3:11–12, 14:6, 18:37), Wisdom teaches people what is of God (Wisdom of Solomon 9:17), utters truth (Proverbs 8:6-7), and leads people to life with God (Proverbs 8:35, 9:6). The symbols of bread, wine, and water and the invitation to eat and drink relate Jesus to Wisdom (John 4:13–15, 6:35, 51ff—cf. Proverbs 9:2-5; Sirach 24:19–21). Wisdom literature also offers parallels to virtually every aspect of the Word described in the Prologue to John. Raymond Brown asserts, "Jesus is divine Wisdom, pre-existent, but now come among [people] to teach them and give them life."[25]

The Wisdom Christology of the New Testament continued to develop during the patristic period. Wisdom and Word were understood as names for Christ, and biblical Wisdom texts were cited in asserting the pre-existence of Christ and the role of Christ in creation. Origen wrote, "Whatever, therefore, we have predicated of the Wisdom of God, will be appropriately applied and understood of the Son of God, in virtue of his being the Life, and the Word . . . for all these titles are derived from His power and operations."[26] Tertullian also noted the equivalence of Wisdom and Word: "[it is] evident that it is one and the same power which is in one place described under the name of Wisdom, and in another passage under the appellation of the Word."[27] Defending the equality of the Son with the Father, Augustine acknowledged the equivalence of Wisdom and Word: "[the Son] was not sent in respect to any inequality of power, or substance, or anything that in Him was not equal to the Father . . . for the Son is the Word of the Father, which is also called His wisdom."[28]

Wisdom did not disappear altogether in the Middle Ages but was manifest in various forms. She was honored in the great cathedral of Hagia Sophia ("Holy Wisdom") in Constantinople, where she was associated with Christ and eventually also with Mary. Some medieval writers continued to identify Wisdom with Christ. But elements of personified Wisdom appear as well in devotion to Mary, in writings about Holy Mother Church, and in the figures of Lady Philosophy and Charity.[29] A Votive Mass attributed to Alcuin of York honors divine Wisdom who is an agent of creation, revelation and salvation. This Mass remained among the Votive Masses in medieval Roman missals but was not included in the 1570 missal, which remained the official liturgy of the Roman Catholic Church until the reforms of the Second Vatican Council in the 1960s.[30]

The supplemental materials draw upon this rich heritage from Scripture and Christian tradition to introduce into contemporary liturgical prayer the figure of divine Wisdom. Canticles from the Hebrew Wisdom tradition express human yearning for wisdom from God ("A Song of Pilgrimage," Sirach 51:13–16, 20b–22) and extol the role of Wisdom in salvation history ("A Song of Wisdom," Wisdom of Solomon 10:15–19, 20b–21). A eucharistic prayer presented to the 1991 General Convention made extensive use of biblical depictions of Wisdom, but this prayer was rejected by the Convention. Wisdom reappeared in a new eucharistic prayer introduced in 1997 (and approved by the General Convention). Although Wisdom is not the predominant image in the prayer, Word and Wisdom are parallel, and Wisdom is identified as agent of creation.

Pronouns

Particularly striking in the Wisdom canticles is the inclusion of the feminine pronoun. It is the most explicit indication that God can be understood not only in masculine terms but also in feminine. Although feminine pronouns were acceptable in canticles, people were not ready to accept feminine pronouns in the proposed Wisdom eucharistic prayer, perhaps because eucharistic prayers are so central to their experience of worship. Eucharistic prayers give thanks to God by recalling God's work in creation and salvation history, particularly the redemptive work of Jesus, and people respond strongly to any change.

As a result of the rejection of the Wisdom eucharistic prayer, there emerged a tacit consensus that we should avoid gendered pronouns altogether when speaking of the divine. The third paragraph of the Nicene Creed returns to the relative pronoun "who" in reference to the Holy Spirit. Eucharistic prayers address God as "you" (as do Prayer Book texts) and make limited use of masculine pronouns when recounting the work of the incarnate Jesus. As part of the less rigid approach in *Enriching Our Worship 1*, some of the New Testament canticles use masculine pronouns (though efforts were made to limit their use), and the canticles from Julian of Norwich mix masculine pronouns with references to God and Jesus as mother. As with the Wisdom canticles, the pronouns are taken from the source material.

The English Language Liturgical Consultation (ELLC) took a different approach to the problem of pronouns in its new translations of the canticles "The Song of Mary" and "The Song of Zechariah." While the texts of these canticles in Luke use third-person pronouns to refer to God, the ELLC translation recast the texts using the second-person "you." Many psalms praise God both by indirect address, using the third person, and direct address, "you." The forms of Hebrew poetry are fluid, and it is not uncommon to find both forms within the same psalm (e.g., Psalms 18, 66, 97, 138, 145). The ELLC materials also cite the liturgical precedent of the *Sanctus*, in which the biblical "his glory" (Isaiah 6:3) has for centuries been rendered "your glory."[31] A similar shift from third to second person was made in the first verse of the Morning Psalm 67, introduced in *Supplemental Liturgical Materials* in 1991, and in *Enriching Our Worship 1*, in an alternative version of the invitatory psalm *Venite*.

The use of second-person pronouns to address the Holy One allows liturgical prayer to retain personal reference to God without the attribution of gender. But the use of pronouns continues to be an important matter in the development of new liturgical materials. Careful writers can provide texts which do not use gendered pronouns and read smoothly as prayer. On the other hand, merely avoiding masculine pronouns in new liturgical texts will not enable a re-imaging of God who is personal and yet beyond gender. The new texts must also provide an abundance of imagery which can enliven prayer and enable a fuller comprehension of the divine mystery.

TREASURES NEW AND OLD

THE DEVELOPMENT OF SUPPLEMENTAL LITURGICAL MATERIALS has been a process of exploring the riches of Scripture and Christian tradition in order to find images and language which engage and inspire American Christians in the Episcopal Church today. Some masculine images—Father, Son, Lord—are deeply rooted in our tradition. But to the extent that these become our only ways to name God in liturgical prayer, they may also become idolatrous. The remedy chosen has not been one of expunging these images, but rather drawing upon more images that also are part of the tradition.

Thus the supplemental materials enrich the church's liturgical expression while drawing more deeply upon our roots in Scripture and Christian tradition. The multiplicity of texts reflects the understanding that no single prayer or liturgy can adequately express the incomprehensible mystery of God and God's gracious love for humanity and all creation as revealed in salvation history. By introducing explicitly feminine imagery as well as limiting the use of gendered pronouns, the new texts seek to complement the predominantly masculine language of most traditional liturgical texts.

NOTES

[1] The Girl Scout Promise currently reads, "On my honor, I will try: To serve God and my country, To help people at all times. . . ."

[2] Charles P. Price for the Standing Liturgical Commission, *Introducing the Draft Proposed Book*, Prayer Book Studies 29 (New York: Church Hymnal Corporation, 1976), p. 26. This discussion of inclusive language is part of a section entitled "Use of Contemporary Language."

[3] Ibid., p. 27.

[4] Booklet printed by Church Hymnal Corporation, New York, for the Standing Liturgical Commission, 1987.

[5] *The Blue Book, Supplement to the Report of the Standing Liturgical Commission*, 1988.

[6] New York: Church Hymnal Corporation, 1989.

[7] New York: Church Hymnal Corporation, 1991; expanded edition, 1996.

[8] New York: Church Publishing Incorporated, 2000. Subsequent to the release of *Enriching Our Worship 2*, the original *Enriching Our Worship* was reissued unchanged as *Enriching Our Worship 1*.

[9] "Supplemental Liturgical Texts," *The Blue Book, Supplement to the Report of the Standing Liturgical Commission*, 1988, p. 98.

[10] Jean Campbell, OSH, "The Feminine as Omitted, Optional, or Alternative Story: A Review of the Episcopal Eucharistic Lectionary," in Ruth A. Meyers, ed., *How Shall We Pray?* Liturgical Studies 2 (New York: Church Hymnal Corporation, 1994), pp. 57–68.

[11] "Supplemental Liturgical Texts," *The Blue Book*, 1988, p. 99.

[12] English Language Liturgical Consultation, *Praying Together* (Norwich CT: Canterbury Press, 1988); see pp. xii–xiii for a discussion of inclusive language.

[13] Mary Rose D'Angelo, "Abba and 'Father': Imperial Theology and the Jesus Traditions," *Journal of Biblical Literature* 111 (1992) 611–630; idem, "Theology in Mark and Q: Abba and 'Father' in

Context," *Harvard Theological Review* 85 (1992) 149–174. See also Elizabeth A. Johnson, *She Who Is* (New York: Crossroad, 1992), pp. 79–82; Ruth A. Meyers, "Principles for Liturgical Language," in *How Shall We Pray?* pp. 87–90; Gail Ramshaw, *God Beyond Gender: Feminist Christian God-Language* (Minneapolis: Fortress Press, 1995), pp. 77–80, 87–88; Sandra M. Schneiders, *Women and the Word* (New York: Paulist Press, 1986), pp. 28–32, 41–49.

[14] *She Who Is*, p. 82.

[15] *Salvation of the Rich Man* 37, in Alexander Roberts and James Donaldson, eds., *The Ante-Nicene Fathers* (10 vols., Buffalo NY: Christian Literature Publishing Company, 1885–1896), II:601 (hereafter cited as *ANF*).

[16] *Homily on the Song of Songs*, cited by J. Robert Wright, "Translating the Tradition," in *How Shall We Pray?* p. 84.

[17] *Showings*, ed. Edmund Colledge and James Walsh (New York, 1978), long text chap. 61, p. 301, cited by Paula Barker, "'Lord, Teach Us to Pray,'" in *How Shall We Pray?* pp. 45–46.

[18] Barker, "'Lord, Teach Us to Pray,'" pp. 46–47. For further discussion of Jesus as mother, see Caroline Walker Bynum, *Jesus as Mother: Studies in the Spirituality of the High Middle Ages* (Berkeley CA: University of California Press, 1982).

[19] See, for example, Alvin F. Kimel, Jr. ed., *Speaking the Christian God: The Holy Trinity and the Challenge of Feminism* (Grand Rapids, MI: Eerdmans, 1992); Donald G. Bloesch, *The Battle for the Trinity: The Debate over Inclusive God-Language* (Ann Arbor MI: Servant Publications, 1985).

[20] See, for example, the discussions in David S. Cunningham, *These Three Are One: The Practice of Trinitarian Theology* (Malden MA, and Oxford: Blackwell Publishers, 1998); Ruth C. Duck and Patricia Wilson-Kastner, *Praising God: The Trinity in Christian Worship* (Louisville KY: Westminster John Knox Press, 1999); Johnson, *She Who Is*, pp. 191–223; Catherine Mowry LaCugna, *God for Us: The Trinity and Christian Life* (San Francisco: HarperSanFrancisco, 1991); Gail Ramshaw, *God Beyond Gender*, pp. 75–87.

²¹ Augustine, "On Christian Doctrine," I.5.5, in Philip Schaff, ed., *A Select Library of the Nicene and Post-Nicene Fathers of the Christian Church* (Buffalo NY: The Christian Literature Company, 1886-1889), 1st ser., II:524 (hereafter cited as *NPNF*).

²² Barker, "'Lord, Teach Us to Pray,'" in *How Shall We Pray?* pp. 51, 55–56.

²³ Johnson, *She Who Is*, pp. 205–211.

²⁴ Ramshaw, *God Beyond Gender*, p. 47.

²⁵ Raymond Brown, *The Gospel According to John (i-xii)*, Anchor Bible 29 (Garden City NY: Doubleday, 1966), p. 524. For further discussion of the Wisdom tradition, see idem, pp. cxxii–cxxv; L. William Countryman, "Biblical Origins of Inclusive Language," in *How Shall We Pray?* pp. 21–25; Paula S. Datsko Barker, "'Lord, Teach Us to Pray,'" in *How Shall We Pray?* pp. 41–43; Johnson, *She Who Is*, pp. 86–100; Schneiders, *Women and the Word*, pp. 51–54.

²⁶ Origen, *De principiis* 1.2.4, in *ANF* IV:247.

²⁷ Tertullian, *Adversus Praxean* 7, in *ANF* III:602.

²⁸ Augustine, *De Trinitate* 4.20.27, in *NPNF*, 1st series, III:83.

²⁹ Barker, "'Lord, Teach Us to Pray,'" in *How Shall We Pray?"* pp. 41–45; Barbara Newman, "The Pilgrimage of Christ-Sophia," *Vox Benedictina* 9 (1992): 8–37.

³⁰ Ruth A. Meyers, "The Wisdom of God and the Word of God: Alcuin's Mass 'of Wisdom,'" in Martin R. Dudley, ed., *Like a Two-Edged Sword: The Word of God in Liturgy and History* (Norwich CT: Canterbury Press, 1995), pp. 39–59.

³¹ *Praying Together*, p. 34.

EXPANSIVE LANGUAGE IN CYBERSPACE

GREGORY HOWE

THE FUTURE WORK of liturgical reform—including possible Prayer Book revision—is here. And it is going to happen via the internet, in ways rather different from what comparatively recent history might suggest.

In the 1920s, a small, insular group of men proceeded along the traditional Anglican "one best way" to deliver what would become The Book of Common Prayer 1928 to a relatively small, rather homogenous General Convention. After the fact, they published an account of what had gone into their work. The process that led eventually to The Book of Common Prayer 1979 was much less exclusive, although admittance into that process at its highest levels still remained somewhat restricted. There were a number of resources made relatively accessible to the church beginning in the mid-1950s, including a series of blue paperback books, "Prayer Book Studies," numbered I–XVI, which constituted very careful, conservative adjustments along the "one best way" toward liturgy. These Prayer Book Studies were issued for study and comment, but on no account were to be used for actual liturgical prayer—although the books were sometimes used in this way. Then in 1967 came the first "Green Book," Prayer Book Studies XVII, *The Liturgy of the Lord's Supper*, approved for study *and* use, and which attempted to insert a certain linguistic duality into the "one best way" by combining a deliberately archaic form of language in reference to God with a more contemporary style in reference to people and their circumstances (after the fashion of the Revised Standard Version of the Bible, which had been published several decades before).

For some, it was too much, for others, too little. The Standing Liturgical Commission had suggested *their* "one best way," but certain bishops had other ideas. Indeed, some bishops were so opposed to the liturgy or its proposed schedule of trial use that some Episcopalians found themselves forbidden to use the material at all. In the meantime, a series of national conferences jointly sponsored by the Standing Liturgical Commission and Associated Parishes provided opportunities for the church to listen to and interact with outstanding liturgists (and SLC members) Terry Holmes, Charles Price, and Boone Porter at the top of their form. Whether these gatherings exerted real influence upon Prayer Book revision is open to debate, but, at the time, it was both fun and energizing for those of us who attended; we debated with Bonnel Spencer, a brother in the Order of the Holy Cross and chair of the Drafting Committee on Christian Initiation, about his vision of a return to the ancient practices that unified Baptism and Confirmation into one Christian initiation; and we listened to Terry Holmes's plea for the full participation of children at the communion table; scandals then, generally accepted norms now.

The early 1970s saw a major surge of print media with more Prayer Book Studies for trial use: the "Green Book," the "Zebra Book," "Son of Zebra," and finally the *Draft Proposed Book of Common Prayer*, presented to the General Convention of 1976. During the course of almost a week of long meetings with representatives of the Standing Liturgical Commission (SLC), the Joint Legislative Committee of General Convention examined the *Draft Proposed Book* in careful detail. The process leading up to publication of the *Draft Proposed Book* had involved more than 250 people—members of the SLC, members of various "drafting committees," and a significant network of reader-consultants. These reader-consultants—chosen quite inclusively—nonetheless were given very exclusive instructions: read and comment on the texts but share them with absolutely no one; there even was a special term for this restricted access: "embargoed." In spite of all the questionnaires and hundreds of voluntary comments, the carefully managed process was "top-down" nonetheless.

I received embargoed copies of several proposed texts. Among them was the proposed rite for the ordination of deacons. One of our most gifted scholars—among the people working on this particular liturgy—was searching for a powerful, contemporary symbol to be given to ordinands along with the New Testament. He had settled on the transmission of a towel. With some trepidation, I responded by suggesting that for many of the lay participants the donation of towels would be associated, primarily, with athletic trainers and upscale washroom attendants. The towels disappeared from the final draft.

The meetings between the SLC and the Joint Legislative Committee finally produced thirteen single-spaced pages of suggested revisions. Some SLC members became convinced that these last-minute changes would kill the *Draft Proposed Book*. Since the House of Bishops had withdrawn from the legislative process to seek enlightenment and peace on the fractious issue of the ordination of women, the revised Prayer Book proposal came to the House of Deputies. The overwhelming vote for the acceptance of the *Draft Proposed Book of Common Prayer*, as amended, surprised most of those who had been involved in the process (and shattered the credibility of the leadership of the organized center of opposition to Prayer Book revision, the Society for the Preservation of the [1928] Book of Common Prayer). In the end, the Prayer Book committee of the House of Deputies—an unusually large group of church members whose only real scholar was the late Massey Shepherd and who represented a wide spectrum of taste and opinion—did what they needed to do on behalf of their parent body. In a modest and somewhat accidental way, this chain of events represented a new sort of grassroots initiative in the life of the Episcopal Church.

Not all the surprises at the 1976 Convention were so pleasant. One promising initiative of the *Draft Proposed Book* was the bracketing of the *filioque* clause in the Nicene Creed, which would make the recitation of the words "and the Son" in the phrase "proceeded from the Father and the Son" optional in certain circumstances. This step—relatively minor to the average Episcopalian—was essential to bettering ecumenical relations with the Orthodox churches, for whom this late "accretion" was a grievous disruption to the delicate balance of trinitarian theology. One member of the legislative committee sat through all pre-convention meetings and nearly a week of regular committee meetings without a negative word; then, as the vote approached, he got up on the floor of the House of Deputies and denounced the proposal, suggesting that it would do grave damage to our relations with Methodists and Presbyterians (neither of whom was known to make much use of the Nicene Creed at the time). His impassioned speech moved a sufficient number of deputies to create a majority of House members who were worried about offending Methodists and Presbyterians, and the brackets were removed in the 1979 Prayer Book—losing an opportunity for slightly more cordial relations with some of the oldest Christian churches.

A survey of the long course of liturgical renewal by the Episcopal Church—before, during, and after the settlement of The Book of Common Prayer 1979—reveals three primary perspectives. First, there is a large, relatively flexible, middle constituency, willing to try something new, if not too extreme, and comfortable with the slow—some would say glacial—pace of liturgical development in the Episcopal Church. Then there is a minority on one side who have always accorded The Book of Common Prayer an iconic status that extends symbolically beyond the church into American society as a whole; these people see the Prayer Book's codification of the church's faith and liturgy as a constant in an ever-changing and most inconstant world. On the other side of our spectrum is another minority, for whom we never go far enough or fast enough in our attempts to provide an adequate platform from which to evangelize the unchurched and the disenfranchised or to satisfy the restless. Neither of these minorities can control the church's liturgical agenda by themselves, but—acting in unintended concert—they can limit what becomes possible.

The social dynamic that occurs between these two groups, as they relate to our Church as a whole, plays a large but poorly understood role in our deliberations together. The best characterization and analysis of it that I know is by someone who is examining, not the church, but American social trends in general. Virginia Postrel—writing from a libertarian perspective in her book *The Future and Its Enemies*[1]—suggests "abandoning traditional political categories" and proposes some new ones: "dynamists— those who accept and promote innovation," and "stasists—who favor a regulated, engineered world." With the explosion of information and technical innovation, she argues, "central planning bodies are impotent; only freedom, even chaos will do." By promoting open practices, she says, "societies will progress; by squelching them, they will go the way of centrally planned governments." One of Postrel's major points—modeled along the lines of "everything that rises must converge"—is that the old Right, chronically distrustful of innovation, is finding common cause with the remnants of the old Left, who tend to want to exercise close, top-down control of any innovations. Thus, Postrel perceives an alliance which tends to discourage innovation and presumes to exercise tight executive control over whatever may be permitted—in short, a union of reaction and technocracy, dedicated to the suppression and micro-management of change.

Postrel's central concern is with the internet, which she envisions as a magic carpet that no clamp-down on innovation or technocratic organizational scheme can control. Along the way in her analysis of this revolutionary new communications tool, she makes some points which ought to be of interest to the church in terms of liturgical renewal and the identification of useful new language.

When initially presented as the *Draft Proposed Book* of 1976, the document that would eventually become The Book of Common Prayer 1979 was condemned by our stasists as unacceptably radical, accepted by the majority of Episcopalians, and quietly scorned by our dynamists as too timid. There were indeed enough new things in the mix to cause certain people alarm: line by line, the 1979 Prayer Book is markedly different from the 1928 Prayer Book in the style of diction used (the language sounds much more like the language spoken in America in the later half of the twentieth century); moreover, the 1979 Prayer Book emphasis upon the centrality of the public prominence of the rites of Baptism and the Holy Eucharist marks a significant departure from the largely nineteenth-century faith and practice of its predecessor. But others—looking around at a rapidly changing world—considered the new Prayer Book a more conservative product, pitched too comfortably within the boundaries of the unique Scottish-American tradition that was its primary foundation and influence.

In fact, the new book *was* conservative in some regards, so much so that it missed the next big thing: "inclusive" or gender-neutral language. Inclusive language was an attempt to take the edge off ecclesiastical patriarchy—which made it difficult for many people to connect with God—by using gender-neutral pronouns and a wider range of metaphors when referring to the persons of the Trinity. Other Anglican provinces, as well as Lutherans, Methodists, and Presbyterians in this country were about to produce inclusive-language worship materials, which made our "new" Prayer Book look somewhat dated. A few years after its distribution, I was upbraided at a reception in Rome by a futurist Benedictine monk, because *my* church had missed the perfect opportunity to add inclusive language to its liturgy.

As the Episcopal Church scrambled to play catch-up, we learned about the downside of this next new thing. An early key principle was "extended metaphor"—metaphors that focus, for example, on God's role in creation: Creator, Maker, Author; but sometimes these metaphors extended so far that it became difficult to make a significant connection between beginning and end, as when our search for feminine imagery led us to fixate on "Wisdom" and then on "Logos" and eventually on what almost became a divine feminine principle, thereby seeming to refute the point that God is beyond gender. As language about God became more neutral and diverse, the divine became transcendent in a way that precluded its being very immanent (which more or less left us right back where we started, with many people finding it difficult to establish a close relationship with God). In our attempts to free the Holy Trinity from the gender presumptions of the English language, we managed to confuse ontological issues with mere job descriptions such as "Redeemer" or "Creator." Consequently we almost lost the most compelling statements of the saving power of the incarnation and atonement of Jesus Christ.

Early attempts at inclusive language—in Prayer Book Studies issued shortly after the 1979 Prayer Book—did much to include those among us (especially women) who previously had not been able to identify fully with the conspicuously masculine God of our Scriptures and liturgies. But even these inclusive materials still presented a major problem of omission; only this omission was subtler, harder to name and point to. From 1985 to 1994 our efforts in inclusive language tended to concentrate on changing specific words in specific texts (what a colleague has called "liturgy by white-out"), but in the process we missed something even more important. We tended to ignore the context—in the largest cultural sense—of our liturgies and our worship, presuming that if we fixed the words correctly, we would achieve appropriate cultural accommodations for everybody.

Our worship needs to include and be seen to include everyone, but this sometimes gets played out in ways that manage to be "inclusive" without being truly "expansive." A large urban parish can work hard at becoming inclusive—with worship services in many different languages—without ever integrating the speakers of those different languages into one church community.

One of my favorite illustrations of cultural diversity comes, not from an Episcopal model, but from the life of a "typical" Roman Catholic parish in lower Delaware. It started as a small parish, serving the needs of a Catholic minority in the midst of a significant WASP majority, but then industrial displacement and international population shifts in the second half of the twentieth century multiplied the size of the Roman Catholic community many times over. One of the most dramatic images of this shift comes as part of a major civic spring festival. As a fundraiser, the parish puts on an international food festival. A spacious gym is filled with the multicultural food offerings of the members of the parish. There is German food, Italian food, Irish food, Filipino food, Polish food, and Vietnamese food. The whole community (including many more ethnic groups not represented at the food festival) comes and has a very good time. Everyone is aware of—and proud of—their diversity, but the important thing to notice about this parish is that they tend *not* to segregate into separate communities, especially in their worship. With the exception of one Spanish Mass, all these ethnic subdivisions worship together with reasonable comfort in English.

In order to become truly expansive, we must become responsible for the ways in which we are seen and known by others. A Eucharist service in English does not necessarily put off someone who is Dominican or Vietnamese—that is, unless the English being used is the liturgical equivalent of cryptography. A number of great minds, such as William F. Buckley, Jr., publisher of the magazine *National Review*, have used their considerable verbal skills to try to freeze us in place at a late stage of the 1928 Prayer Book, as though we are the custodians of a sacred cultural icon without which Anglo civilization, as we know it, would wither away. People such as Buckley—who is not Episcopalian and who would never use *any* edition of The Book of Common Prayer in its true context of worship—condemned us with great passion during the revision of the 1928 Prayer Book for presuming to tamper with such a classic of literature. For them the Episcopal Church is the guardian of an exquisitely beautiful museum piece. Our tradition represents a kind of abstract beauty, a sort of platonic ideal of liturgical and cultural discourse, which they defend for a wide variety of sociopolitical—rather than strictly religious—reasons.

If we are content to be museum-keepers, we accept a vocation to protect an item of great beauty, but what does that have to do with the imperatives of the Gospel? Aren't we sending the message that spreading the Gospel isn't quite as important to us as the beautiful, even glorious literature (and other magnificent treasures) entrusted to us? Our tradition does indeed greatly value these things, but there also are many people out there to be reached, and the language of our liturgy must help us in that aim, not hinder us.

"Inclusive language" represents an attempt to open up the liturgical structure to include those who saw themselves excluded because of gender. "Expansive language" is an attempt to maintain gender integrity and move on to open up a wider range of cultural issues and opportunities. This is not quite as revolutionary as it may sound. Early in the history of our church, a surprising mixture of Dutch, French, German, and Swedish people—as well as a significant number of African Americans—chose to become Episcopalians. True, some of that was the result of deals cut between European princes or the result of the grim reality of slavery, but for most it was or became a matter of free choice, as a natural part of the religious accommodation people elected for themselves in the New World. Are we as open and accessible to new Americans today as we were two or three centuries ago? Can we become more accessible now, without ignoring or rejecting our own history? We certainly need to loosen up in our attitudes toward languages other than English. Other parts of the Anglican Communion have produced Prayer Books that are multilingual—with exciting results; not separate translations of the Prayer Book, but the languages of different peoples side by side. This approach to language is expansive in the best meaning of the word.

Expansive language, as it is now before this church, is an attempt to discover more such applications (and their remarkable ramifications). Our severest critics denounce expansive language as a secular cultural accommodation—the church trying to act too much like the world—and it is one of the most important questions about expansive language. Is the claim of secular accommodation true? The church is always susceptible to "the ways of the world," but consider this stirring exhortation in the Epistle to the Romans: "Do not be conformed to this world, but be transformed by the renewal of your minds, so that you may discern what is the will of God" (Romans 12:2). Those who work with expansive language do so because they understand this to be a discernment process to comprehend the will of God for our time and place, to illuminate the presence of God among us as clearly as possible.

In an important essay on canon law in the Episcopal Church, Leigh Axton Williams demonstrates a modern twist on St. Paul's exhortation, quoting a favorite phrase from a frequently underrated Roman Catholic leader, Pope Paul VI: *novus habitus mentis*—new habit of mind—a point modeled constantly and courageously by that quiet hero of liturgical reform.[2] Discussing this new habit of mind and its possible application in the life of the Episcopal Church, Williams notes:

> All liturgy expresses, in part, our human desire to experience the Divine presence, and liturgical law intends to preserve this authentic expression of the Church's self-revelation (rather than solely to govern the activities of our worship) . . . then examining liturgical rites according to a disciplined process of inquiry should display to us more clearly the mystery of Christ that imbues liturgical rite and the spirit, the expression, of the holy things they signify. This should draw us into deeper and more intimate contact with the living God . . .[3]

Thus the foundation of expansive language is not a matter of secular accommodation but a disciplined process of inquiry, a theological quest to draw closer to God, in our time and place, within our forms of worship.

There is also a practical and pastoral consideration which informs our quest for expansive language. The Episcopal Church survives and grows in significant part due to a stream of adults drawn to it from ecclesiastical elsewheres. Some come from backgrounds that are highly participatory but somewhat disorderly, others from situations presumably free but not very participatory.

From either side, a vision of dignity, order, and participation can be enormously attractive.

For these very reasons, some would argue that we should not change anything. After all, the excitement and enthusiasm of these pilgrims are some of the most joyful aspects of being an Episcopalian. Yet anyone who has had pastoral responsibility for these hopeful seekers has also experienced their frustration with what appears to them a bewildering multitude of books to use—always jumping back and forth between them—and then standing, sitting, kneeling, standing again. As new members live into our fellowship, they often find themselves bewildered, confused, even embarrassed by it all. To help matters where I served, I tried to match new people with experienced members and even wrote a "Sunday Morning Survival Guide"—a little pamphlet that reassured newcomers and urged them to relax and not worry so much about whether they were "getting it right" the first few visits. We really do need to be more accessible than we are; and this goes beyond matters of church etiquette—whether one is crossing oneself at the proper time. We have a whole private language, and it is glorious! It even helped to bring many of us back to the church; but literary evangelism such as this, to be successful, presupposes a certain level—and even a certain tradition—of education steeped in the English classics of Tudor and Elizabethan poetry and prose. But to those who have been educated otherwise, our liturgy and our community is frequently closed.

"Expansive language" following as it did upon the heels of "inclusive language" might make the stasists among us wonder, "Are we merely in love with the new?" It would be most unfortunate if expansive language was attractive primarily because it was new (which would mean that we have turned our backs on a linguistic heritage of immense beauty merely for the amusement that novelty affords!). To be authentic, expansive language should be the work of liturgists who model themselves upon the scribe in Jesus' parable: "every scribe who has been trained for the kingdom of heaven is like the master of a household who brings out of his treasure what is new and what is old" (Matthew 13:52). To write expansive language is, ideally, to do two things at once: to bring forward and conserve the best of a great tradition, while presenting new words and new images for our time.

We are the heirs of a very special estate. The Scottish-American tradition in which we stand represents the oldest self-supporting, most democratic, nonestablishment part of Anglicanism. We are part of a happy few who need not spend time and energy reacting to the English models of 1552–1662. We have been standing on our own feet, in our own place for a significant period of time, and it is a precious heritage of freedom that we would be foolish to discard.

The current work of expansive language—which became the responsibility in 1997 of the Standing Commission on Liturgy and Music, newly configured from the Standing Liturgical Commission and the Standing Commission on Church Music—has been largely a matter of trying to follow the principle of valuing both the old and the new. In the case of *Enriching Our Worship 1*, which was the first major contribution from liturgists working fully in "expansive"—rather than "inclusive"—mode, a small group was sent off with a shopping list and instructions, and told to come back with finished proposals. These were accepted with minor revisions and forwarded to the General Convention. Once in the legislative process, the proposals appeared to be sufficiently noncontroversial as to move quietly to the Consent Calendar and were approved without debate.

Recent work on alternative rites for the sick and dying and the restoration of a distinct rite for the burial of a child—which culminated in 2000 in the publication of *Enriching Our Worship 2*—proceeded in similar fashion. Since both *Enriching Our Worship 1* and *Enriching Our Worship 2* were very low-budget operations, we had only about fifty reader-consultants (after all, these are optional, alternative rites that tend not to attract the ample resources that the church would give to revision of The Book of Common Prayer). In theory, manuscripts are still guarded in semi-secrecy until the time of publication, but in fact much of the material for *Enriching Our Worship 2* appeared on the internet at least a year in advance of the 2000 General Convention.

The internet offers some exciting possibilities for the future of liturgical revision. Most significantly, it offers an alternative to the formats now available: traditionally bound printed materials (which evince stability and a certain formality), printed ring-binder materials (which facilitate frequent, inexpensive updating—as with government and corporate policy manuals), and CD-ROMs (which can be very economical). Each of these distribution alternatives has some drawbacks. Printing costs have risen dramatically since the last Prayer Book Studies were published; and, as noted in the introduction to *Enriching Our Worship 1*, high production costs for *Supplemental Liturgical Materials* resulted in a print run so modest that the book was out of print and unobtainable before many congregations had learned of its existence. Ring-binder materials carry, for many, an undesirable air of transience, and they do not stand up well to heavy use. As for the supposed economic dividends of issuing new liturgical materials on CD-ROM, second and third iterations can indeed be remarkably inexpensive to produce, but—unless a given offering is likely to be a work-in-progress, with several subsequent revised editions to follow—the enormous start-up costs for developing and testing the very first CD-ROM iteration can end up being more expensive than other options. Finally, all three of these alternatives share another disadvantage, one that is built in to any liturgical revision that proceeds without benefit of the internet: the authors, revisers, and editors of supplemental materials are volunteers whose busy schedules can slow production to a crawl; and because these volunteers are not project staff members who are gathered in one place, these volunteers must be brought together at enormous expense.

Texts shared via the internet could be made available quickly and widely, at the lowest possible cost. All participants in the process can be brought together at a moment's notice, no matter where they may be, and at little or no cost. And because materials that are posted to websites somehow tend to be considered less "final" than versions promulgated by other modes of distribution, those developing the materials tend to be less anxious about letting go of their work. Versions clearly designated as "draft" or "preliminary" may be posted at any and all stages of the process; and because everything is generally available and access is no longer seen as privileged, there could be a higher volume of interest and response from the widest possible blend of sources in the church.

The potential of liturgical dialogue on the internet also suggests some attractive possibilities in terms of Postrel's dynamist principles:

1. Dynamist principles allow individuals (or groups of individuals) to act on their own knowledge, to extend the limits of what any authority can know.
2. Dynamist principles can be applied to small, local groups or communities, allowing them to combine in many ways. Such bottom-up building is adaptable. While stasists create brittle systems by trying to specify every detail in advance, this dynamist principle allows for flexibility.
3. Dynamist principles permit credible, understandable, enduring, and enforceable commitments. Postrel makes a major distinction and contrast between relationships founded on status (frequently unequal and unpredictable) and those founded on contract—which encourage competition without vulnerability.
4. Dynamist principles tend to protect criticism, competition, and feedback.

Thus, dynamist process

> invests no one with decisive power, assumes that no one is omniscient or even particularly wise. . . . It acknowledges human differences and permits diverse approaches. It recognizes that most ideas will fail . . . and turns that weakness into a powerful lever for progress. "There is no way to find the best decision except to try as many designs as possible and discard the failures," writes Freeman Dyson. "Trial and error understands that life is unpredictable."

This sounds like a good recipe for authentic expansive language for the Episcopal Church. However, as Postrel also points out in her remarks about religious groups, we tend to be comfortable in our neighborhood; many have no wish to leave it, and others react very negatively to any attempt to change it. Against that, Presiding Bishop Frank T. Griswold noted in one of his homilies several years ago: "We must always drive ourselves to be connected to a community which is larger than our preferred community because that larger community is in fact where Christ most fully is to be found."

Since 1928, the process of liturgical renewal in the Episcopal Church has moved from a tightly controlled, top-down technocratic mode, with relatively little input—except when loud howls of dismay precipitated shifts in direction—to a slightly more open, still reasonably controlled, largely top-down mode. We reached bottom in the 1980s, when the SLC generally ceased to acknowledge or respond to any unofficial questions or suggestions. Since then, a much higher degree of response and accountability has been restored. All this is somewhat understandable. On a practical level, those officially charged with the church's liturgical enterprise are in a strict sense accountable only to the General Convention and its interim leaders. Moreover, this is a small group of volunteers with relatively little spare time or support resources. On a more abstract level, The Book of Common Prayer is our identity and direction in a way that few other widely distributed liturgical texts are for any other worshiping community. Given this heady responsibility placed upon the revisers of our liturgy, we should not be too surprised when some of them become overly cautious during the process.

Recently, there has been much sincere frustration and regret within the Standing Commission on Liturgy and Music due to the relative lack of grassroots input. Yet, since average members of the Episcopal Church are reasonably smart and recognize technocratic control when they see it, there has been little real incentive for feedback until recently, especially since the advent of the internet. Things are changing, but it is likely to take a while longer to convince the person in the pew of that fact. If our liturgy is to become an authentic mirror of our widening multicultural identity, then we must find more effective ways to present our cross-cultural realities. The internet may prove to be the vehicle which will assist a necessary cross-cultural conversation within the Episcopal Church and help us to find truly expansive language.

Where are we going? The Book of Common Prayer 1979 broke with the rigid "one best way" tradition, providing legitimacy for choice (at least in some things), which is vitally important as we move toward the possibility of more expansive and culturally inclusive liturgy (for which breadth of choice is essential). Choice, thanks to the 1979 Prayer Book, is now constitutionally legitimate (as with the choices Rite I or Rite II; Eucharistic Prayer A, B, C, or D; Prayers of the People Forms I, II, III, et al.). But do these choices make us truly catholic? Yes, suggests the historical data from the church in its first millennium, which had an abundance of choice in liturgy—choices that changed from community to community. Yet the dynamism of choices found in the church in its first millennium is frightening to many; it isn't abundance—it's chaos. No one is ever sure where it is going, and no one really seems to be in charge. Still, if we are going to be seriously multi-cultural, there is no one small group of experts who can know exactly what the rest of us should do.

One of the basic religious impulses is to the familiar. We want to live in our neighborhood, where the familiar is valued and preserved. As previously noted, the 1979 Prayer Book was far more conservative and traditional than its most savage critics would ever let on. The Book of Common Prayer 1979 was faithful to our church's particular birthright—the Scottish-American tradition—in ways that make us virtually unique in Anglicanism. Recent revisions in the prayer books of the churches in England and New Zealand—by marked contrast—were not congruent with their most basic traditions, all of which lead directly back to the "classical" British book of 1662. For example, the Church of England's *Alternative Service Book* 1980 grafted onto the end of the eucharistic prayer a continental Roman Catholic responsory—a mode not seen in previous Anglican usage; also included are the non-Anglican congregational responses for the Roman offertory, which, to Anglican ears, seem to anticipate the eucharistic prayer. As for *A New Zealand Prayer Book* 1988, which caused such a stir in our own church when it was released, it maintained a certain imported Calvinism, albeit in a kinder, gentler presentation. Examples might include a reluctance to pray for the dead; to offer, present or bring before God the bread and wine in relation to the *anamnesis* of the eucharistic prayer; or to connect the eucharistic elements with the sacrifice of our Savior Jesus Christ—all of which are key themes in the Scottish-American tradition from Laud's Book of Common Prayer of 1637 to The Book of Common Prayer 1979.

We are fortunate to have a very solid foundation on which to build. We have retained the heart of what has been ours from the beginning and opened up a variety of new possibilities so that there is no one best way, and a number of alternatives are equally legitimate. What then should we build in the future, and how shall we build it? Will we always have a Book of Common Prayer?

To take the last question first, I hope we will have a Book of Common Prayer always. It is our identity and direction in a unique way, and I cannot imagine anything else that could provide an adequate replacement. In Postrel's terms, it is the contract which binds together local congregations, dioceses, ECUSA, and the Anglican Communion. It is our indispensable given. What kind of Prayer Book should we have? There are two obvious choices. One would look very much like what we have now, with more culturally expansive language. Another possibility, much discussed in some quarters these days, would offer an expansion of "An Order for Celebrating the Holy Eucharist" (see The Book of Common Prayer, pp. 400–405)—a series of agendas or directories, with some required texts and indicated parts of others. (This model may have been inspired by Lambeth Conference recommendations which, since 1958, have suggested that the way forward in inter-Anglican liturgy is a matter of unity of structure rather than full liturgical texts.) This possibility sounds exciting, since it would give the broadest possible scope for the application of local wisdom. Yet there are potential problems.

For one thing, would the rest of the Anglican Communion recognize such a book of lists from the Episcopal Church as a Book of Common Prayer? Just how "common" could the results of such an arrangement be? And just how practical, on a day to day basis, is a worship book of lists? Wouldn't liturgy planning with such a list be harder, not easier? Worship outlines of this nature can indeed make for exciting, powerful new opportunities in liturgy, but only if they rest securely upon our church's solid foundation. But, as we move toward a model of ordained ministry that bypasses expensive, time-consuming seminary training in favor of programs of study that will get priests into the field faster, we may be producing clergy with a limited knowledge of our heritage and our liturgical history, clergy who cannot mix the stability of the old with the excitement of the new in the right proportions to produce good liturgy. Moreover, one of the earliest principles of The Book of Common Prayer was to put, not just rites, but a rule of faith in the hands of the whole church. Any collection of structures and partials texts puts control, not only of rites, but also of the rule of faith, firmly and completely in the hands of the clergy—a result which would provide a major surprise to Archbishop Cranmer, who sought to provide a level playing field for clergy and laity.

But there is a third way. Imagine a Book of Common Prayer with a significant choice of full texts, adjusted and refined by major grassroots input, with an absolute minimum of directions and rubrics (as demonstrated in the Scottish Episcopal trial books of the mid-1980s) so that local congregations would have maximum freedom for the significant gestures, ceremonies, and traditions of their own cultural situation, with the least pressure to be bound by those of another time and place. A corollary benefit of a truly expansive Book of Common Prayer might be the abolition of the many "wee bookies"—those very elaborate service bulletins which have sprung up in part as a reaction to the conservatism of the 1979 Prayer Book, but which, unfortunately, do not provide a very broad familiarity with The Book of Common Prayer. A truly expansive Prayer Book would remove a great deal of confusion for our non-Episcopal guests or for Episcopalians visiting unfamiliar parishes. It would also do much to strengthen the catholicity of our church.

We have an exciting opportunity before us—not to be fashionable or politically correct—but to be effectively incarnational as witnesses to our risen and eternal Savior Jesus Christ. As one of the giants of the field, Dom Anscar Chupungco, puts it in *Liturgical Inculturation*:

> How many nations in the world today can claim to be in possession of a culture that has no admixture of other cultures? The question is particularly relevant to multicultural countries like the United States. Though it has an indigenous community, it is a crossroads of ethnic groups from every region of the world. Its constitutive principle, *e pluribus unum*, has created the unusual phenomenon of a truly multiethnic nation wherein the indigenous culture does not constitute the substratum of the entire civilization. . . . We know that cultures are in a continual process of change due to mutual influence encouraged by modern means of communication. . . . Since the Liturgy is a living expression of faith—its cultural elements, with the exception of those that are of divine origin, should likewise be contemporary.[4]

Thus, in the view of this distinguished teacher at the Pontifical Liturgical Institute in Rome—who is Filipino by birth and a Benedictine monk by choice—we stand at an exciting crossroad. Careful, authentic, expansive language, informed by local wisdom and the broadest possible grassroots participation, can provide for this church, out of many, one in Christ. If we elect to turn away from this opportunity, we should also heed the warning that Dom Anscar provides elsewhere: "a liturgy whose cultural pattern differs radically from that of the local Church has to adapt or be pushed to irrelevance."[5]

Those who are charged with the work of expansive language for this church understand their responsibility to be a matter of adaptation rather than replacement. This is an extension of a work long-in-progress, "seeking to keep the happy mean between too much stiffness in refusing, and too much easiness in admitting variations in things once advisedly established."[6] For reasons noted above, it seems useful to propose a shift in the process: to utilize the dramatic technological change offered by the internet to encourage much wider participation in the work of liturgical renewal, so that when the next move to revise The Book of Common Prayer is eventually authorized, a broad range of voices may be heard, and the greatest variety of gifts may be received.

In the end, the Scottish-American tradition celebrated here is much more than particular issues of form and structure in the prayers of the Eucharist. Thomas Talley has noted: "It was only with the Scottish and American revisions of the BCP that the classic structure of the [eucharistic] prayer was restored."[7] Talley is pointing to a structural and technically theological issue. Far more important is the spiritual foundation of the Scottish-American tradition: "an epicletic eucharistic theology that sees all sacraments, the life of the church and the life of all Christians, as the work of the Spirit, who is evoked upon both people and upon bread and wine at every eucharist."[8] It is this wonderful vision which our work struggles to illuminate and which, for true inclusivity, should have the widest possible participation. That is why the proposed next step is a pilgrimage in cyberspace. Then we may celebrate a truly expansive statement of God's presence among us, through the Spirit promised and given by our Savior Jesus Christ.

NOTES

[1] All references to the work of Virginia Postrel are to be found in her book *The Future and Its Enemies: The Growing Conflict Over Creativity, Enterprise, and Progress* (New York: Free Press, 1998).

[2] Leigh Axton Williams, "Reflections on Canon Law and Liturgical Revision: Fostering a *Novus Habitus Mentis* in the Episcopal Church," in Paul V. Marshall and Lesley Northup, eds., *Leaps and Boundaries: The Prayer Book in the 21st Century* (Harrisburg PA: Morehouse Publishing, 1997), p. 60.

[3] Ibid., p. 63.

[4] Anscar Chupungco, *Liturgical Inculturation: Sacramentals, Religiosity, and Catechesis* (Collegeville MN: Liturgical Press, 1992), pp. 16–17.

[5] Ibid., p. 36.

[6] BCP 1789; see BCP 1979, pp. 9–10.

[7] Cited by William R. Crockett, "Eucharistic Theology and Anglican Eucharistic Revision," in David R. Holeton, ed., *Our Thanks and Praise: The Eucharist in Anglicanism Today: Papers from the Fifth International Anglican Liturgical Consultation* (Toronto: Anglican Book Centre, 1998), p. 38.

[8] Ian Paton, "The Scottish Episcopal Church," in *Our Thanks and Praise*, p. 246.

II.
PRAYERS FOR
VARIOUS OCCASIONS

PREFACE TO THE
PRAYERS

ONE OF THE RICHEST RESOURCES of a liturgical church is its calendar. As our worship follows its cycle through the course of each year, the prayers call to mind Christ's coming among us: the Word made flesh; Jesus' ministry, suffering, death, resurrection, and ascension; the reign of God; the holy and undivided Trinity. Simultaneously, they celebrate the history of God's people as recorded in Scripture and in the lives of the church's saints. Finally, they help us recollect the covenant between God and creation: "the vast expanse of interstellar space, galaxies, suns, the planets in their courses, and this fragile earth, our island home," with its seasons of growth and harvest, winter rest and new life:

> All of heaven, stars, earth, waters, day, and night, rejoice now
> for the new and splendid grace given them through Christ,
> for all things were as if dead, buried by oppression and tainted
>   by false use,
> but now are raised in life to praise God;
> hell itself is redeemed, powers of evil trampled down,
> and we are saved.
> —*Eucharistic Prayer from the writings of Anselm of Canterbury*

Experiencing these different levels, we are brought deeper into understanding a triune God who does not stand aloof from creation, but loves what the divine Word brought into being and has made us an Easter people:

> Splendor and honor are yours by right,
> God of all being, your power sustains,
> your endless love restores this broken world.
> Always present with us,
> you bring order out of chaos,
> you fill our emptiness with life.
>
> *—Eucharistic Prayer: New Life, the Lord, the Spirit*

The "Prayers for Various Occasions" offered in this volume are arranged to reflect the church year, the calendar of saints, and various pastoral situations. More "occasional" than the materials in *Enriching Our Worship 1* and *Enriching Our Worship 2*, they are designed to provide new expansive-language resources for study and discussion. Placed in conjunction with the essays in this book, they illustrate some of the principles discussed. Many of these prayers draw their inspiration from the writings of holy women and men of past ages: Anselm of Canterbury, Julian of Norwich, Hildegard of Bingen. One eucharistic prayer draws its imagery from the Celtic tradition. The poetic Advent Bidding—originally created for the National Cathedral in Washington, D.C.—contains a litany in which each petition begins with the words of a familiar Advent hymn. Because of the Christological emphasis in Anglicanism, our prayer must focus especially on the saving action of the eternal Word, "your Wisdom from on high by whom you created all things," as one of the eucharistic prayers in *Enriching Our Worship 1* expresses it. We ask to grow ever closer to Jesus who, though God, became human like us, brought the Good News, healed the sick and suffering as a sign of the reign of God drawn near, died to redeem our sins and conquer death so that we might be born into the eternal life of the Trinity.

At the same time, all these prayers strive for imagery that will speak to the hearts and minds of contemporary worshipers. People need to be able to relate unfamiliar words and metaphors to some context, so that the language expresses *their* prayer as the people of God. "Unfamiliar words (*glossa* in Greek) simply puzzle us," Aristotle wrote. "Ordinary words (*koine*) convey what we know already; it is from metaphor that we can get hold of something new and fresh." For some, a major sense of context will spring from their own life experience; others will look for continuity with biblical and ecclesiastical tradition. Corporate prayer which truly expresses our prayer as God's people operates on many levels, yet all tending toward a common understanding of God's plan of salvation through Jesus Christ and the Church's work in the Holy Spirit. The Rev. Bruce Jenneker—a priest originally from South Africa who is currently co-chair of the Standing Commission on Liturgy and Music—has put this most evocatively. He characterizes the qualities of liturgical spirituality as

> its sacramental heart, the emphasis on beauty and graciousness, the participation of all the worshipers, the interactive nature of liturgical prayer, the engagement of the senses, the involvement of the whole body (sitting, standing, kneeling, walking, greeting, touching, eating, drinking). This way of worship stretches across time and place and race and class.

Most traditional prayers have relied heavily on rural imagery. Today, however, many city dwellers have little experience with the countryside or agricultural metaphors. Yet the Bible does depict urban environments as well as rural. Indeed, the culminating vision of Revelation pictures, not a beautiful garden to mirror Eden, but, instead, the City of God—Jerusalem redeemed. *Gleanings* includes a "Eucharistic Prayer for the City" based on scriptural images and concluding,

> Grant that we may build a city at unity with itself,
> its streets safe to walk in, peace within its walls,
> a river of living water flowing from its mercy-seat,
> your Christ its Governor . . .

In a related vein, another eucharistic prayer—originally composed for the celebration of the Diocese of Delaware's companion relationship with the Diocese of Pretoria in South Africa—forcefully reminds worshipers that our self-imposed boundaries, racial, cultural, or economic, find no place in God's scheme of things:

> You created us to love you with all our heart, and to love each other as ourselves, but we have rejected the wonder of the diversity of races and cultures which you gave us so that we might know you in all your majesty, and we rebel against you by the evil that we do. In Jesus, you bring healing to our world and gather us into one great family. Through the powerful and graceful witness of your saints, you have enriched our vision of the people called together by your love in the redeeming power of our Savior.
> *Glory to God for ever and ever.*

For the Feast of Corpus Christi, we have included "A Pilgrimage of Prayer for Healing the Body of Christ," a liturgy originally conducted as a pilgrimage through the streets of St. Louis, with the pilgrims stopping at six sites where murders had taken place to pray for the victims' souls and listen to readings from various sources including Bishop Dehqani-Tafti of Iran; President of the World Council of Churches, Allen Boesak of South Africa; British liturgist Janet Morley; and the African-American educator W.E.B. Du Bois.

Spirituality is at the heart of worship. During much of the twentieth century, rationalism kept many people away from organized religion: why believe in what cannot be proved? Something has happened, though, in the last three or four decades, to change all that. Today, popular culture burgeons with accounts by people convinced they have glimpsed the afterlife, with stories of miraculous interventions by guardian angels. People hunger for communion with the Divine. They don't merely want to "understand"; they long to "experience." They need to feel their "hearts strangely warmed." Christianity finds itself competing not with rationalists so much as with New Age and with other occult traditions. Now, more than ever, the church needs to make use of its own rich ecstatic tradition. Many themes of the prayers included in *Gleanings* concern the problems faced by our culture; however, they petition God in language which evokes the Christian mysticism of the early church and the medieval monastics:

> Awake, arise, leave behind the darkness of sin, and walk in the light that shines on our path. And as this most marvelous light renews in us the hope of glory to which Christ beckons us, let us have on our hearts all those who see no light, for whom all is darkness and despair. Pray that they too may be illumined by Christ in whom there is no darkness at all, for he is the light of the world.
>
> —*An Advent Bidding*

> Welcome, Christ-Light, long awaited and desired one!
> Give us the courage of your presence
> to transform this world into a place fit for your arrival,
> decked with justice, loving-kindness, and mercy,
> glad with our songs of praise in company with the angels,
> alive with your Holy Spirit.
>
> —*Christmas Candle Prayer*

God of all harmony: you are the music of life, the ground-note
of our being. Hear us, for we have lost our bearings. Heal us
for the sake of your Jesus. Fill our emptiness and center our
souls in you, we pray.

*—A Litany of Healing and Wholeness based
on the writings of Hildegard of Bingen*

As a mother gives her child to suck of her milk,
so our precious Mother Jesus feeds us with himself,
most courteously and tenderly,
with the blessed sacrament,
which is the precious food of true life.
For you, O God, sustain us and all that is,
most mercifully and graciously,
though we are but as a hazelnut in your hand.

—Eucharistic Prayer from the writings of Julian of Norwich

Sister Jean Campbell, OSH, has observed, "The task of the
church is not merely to translate but to find the voice of prayer in
the heart, spirit and mind of the people praying. . . . As the process
unfolds, new questions are raised and new avenues disclosed." As
the Episcopal Church enters a new millennium, *Gleanings*
attempts to further discern the voice of common prayer. We hope
our experiments may inspire yours.

Phoebe Pettingell

THE CHURCH YEAR

ADVENT

AN ADVENT BIDDING

An acolyte stands ready with a taper at the Advent wreath. The advent candles are lit at the reference to "the birth of our Lord and Savior Jesus Christ."
The Presider says

We welcome you in the name of God, who has delivered us from the dominion of darkness and transferred us to the reign of Jesus Christ, the only begotten of God: grace to you, and peace.

We are gathered to proclaim and receive in our hearts the good news of the Advent and so prepare ourselves to celebrate with confidence and joy the birth of our Lord and Savior Jesus Christ. We pray that we may respond in penitence and faith to the glory of God's purposes, and be found ready for the new life we are offered, with its works of justice and its promise of mercy, its blessing and its hope.

Let us in this holy season reflect on the coming of Christ who brings light into the world. In prayer, praise, and song, let us give voice to the hope set forth in the Scriptures: that the kingdom of Christ shall come.

Awake, arise, leave behind the darkness of sin, and walk in the light that shines on our path. And as this most marvelous light renews in us the hope of glory to which Christ beckons us, let us have on our hearts all those who see no light, for whom all is darkness and despair. Pray that they too may be illumined by Christ in whom there is no darkness at all, for he is the light of the world.

AN ADVENT LITANY

The Litanist begins the litany and the People respond.

O God, the loving Source of all life, Giver of light and Fountain of hope,
Have mercy upon us.

O God, the Savior of the world, Redeemer of our sins and Beloved Friend of all,
Have mercy upon us.

O God, sustaining Spirit, Breath of life and Pulse of love,
Have mercy upon us.

O holy, blessed, and glorious Trinity, one God,
Have mercy upon us.

Blessed are you, O Lord our God.
You have come to your people and set them free.

You have raised up for us a mighty Savior,
Born of the house of your servant David.

Blessed is the one who comes in the name of the Lord.
Hosanna in the highest.

To shine on those who dwell in darkness and the shadow of death,
And to guide our feet into the way of peace.

Blessed are you, O Lord our God.
You have come to your people and set them free.

We wait for your loving-kindness, O God,
In the midst of your temple.

The glory of the Lord shall be revealed;
And all flesh shall see it together.

Show us your mercy, O Lord,
And grant us your salvation.

Blessed are you, O Lord our God.
You have come to your people and set them free.

Creator of the stars of night, your people's everlasting light: Look not upon the darkness of our selfish greed, nor leave us in our blindness, but let your marvelous light shine upon us and save us. Come among us, Lord Jesus Christ.
Come, Lord Jesus.

O Christ, Redeemer of us all, we pray you hear us when we call: Support those who are alone, ashamed, and afraid; disturb those who are smug, insensitive, and vain; find those who are lost, diminished, and downhearted. Come among us, Lord Jesus Christ.
Come, Lord Jesus.

In sorrow that the ancient curse should doom to death a universe, you come to set us free from our old bondage to sin and darkness and death; come again and free us from the chains of pride and

hypocrisy, envy and hatred, and prepare in us the way of love. Come among us, Lord Jesus Christ.
Come, Lord Jesus.

You came, O Savior, to set free your own in glorious liberty: Make us bold in the freedom you bring us, daring in the redemption that you offer, that the works of justice and peace, compassion and mercy may be the fruits of our joy. Come among us, Lord Jesus Christ.
Come, Lord Jesus.

When this old world drew on toward night, you came, to bring the kingdom of heaven near to us who had gone far astray from God's plan. Rekindle in us the hope of glory, that with all creation we may wait with eager longing for the fulfillment of God's purposes. Come among us, Lord Jesus Christ.
Come, Lord Jesus.

You came not as a monarch, but as the child of Mary, blameless mother mild, to speak God's love in close companionship, as brother, teacher, friend. Strengthen the bonds of love wherever they bless your people; between parents and children, spouses, kindred, and friends, and let no one be without love or friendship. Come among us, Lord Jesus Christ.
Come, Lord Jesus.

At your great Name, O Jesus, now all knees must bend, all hearts must bow; Gather the scattered Church into your love and make our divisions cease. Unite us with N. our Presiding Bishop, N. our Bishop, all bishops, priests, and deacons, and all your people, in the joyful expectation of your reign. Come among us, Lord Jesus Christ.
Come, Lord Jesus.

All things on earth with one accord, like those in heaven shall call you Lord. Inspire faithfulness in those who know your Name and walk in your Way; open our eyes to your presence with those who call upon God by other names, and reach out to those who choose to live without God. Come among us, Lord Jesus Christ.
Come, Lord Jesus.

Come in your holy might, we pray, redeem us for eternal day: Stir up your power among us so that God's will be done on earth as in heaven. Give wisdom to the leaders of the nations, especially [N.] our President, [N.] our Vice President, the Congress and the Supreme Court, the representatives of the United Nations, [N.] our mayor and the City Council, the government and people of the state of _____. Come among us, Lord Jesus Christ.
Come, Lord Jesus.

Defend us while we dwell below from all assaults of our dread foe. Support the sick, uphold those who do not have the resources for living, deliver those in the crisis of temptation, comfort the dying, and console the bereaved; strengthen those who care for the needy, and call many to minister to those who suffer, so that we might triumph over every evil in the power of your name. Come among us, Lord Jesus Christ.
Come, Lord Jesus.

Savior of the nations, come, and save your people from their sins, forgive us our trespasses we pray, give us true repentance, and the grace of the Holy Spirit to amend our lives. Come among us, Lord Jesus Christ.
Come, Lord Jesus.

Savior of the nations, come, and teach us to live in the marvelous light of your peace, that wars may cease and a spirit of mutual trust, interdependence, and forbearance grow among the peoples. Come among us, Lord Jesus Christ.
Come, Lord Jesus.

Savior of the nations, come, give to us a due sense of God's providence, that we may respect the earth, be faithful stewards of its bounty, and conserve it for those who come after us. Come among us, Lord Jesus Christ.
Come, Lord Jesus.

Savior of the nations, come, and inspire us in our several callings, that we may do the work we do, not for ourselves alone, but for the common good. Come among us, Lord Jesus Christ.
Come, Lord Jesus.

Savior of the nations, come, and make us worthy of our children. You came among us as a little child, to show us the way to God. Enable us to see every child as a precious trust, that no child will be at risk, and all children will have the opportunity to become what you have called them to be. Come among us, Lord Jesus Christ.
Come, Lord Jesus.

Savior of the nations, come, endow our communities with a new sense of fellowship and restore in us the bonds of concord, that our streets may be free of violence, our children secure, and all people live together in peace. Come among us, Lord Jesus Christ.
Come, Lord Jesus.

Savior of the nations, come, and gather into the arms of your everlasting mercy the souls of all the departed, that, with Mary the mother of our Lord [and N.], and all the saints, they may live in your eternal light and peace. Come among us, Lord Jesus Christ.
Come, Lord Jesus.

Savior of the nations, come; grant us your glories to see.
Savior of the nations, come; grant us your glories to see.

Lamb of God, you take away the sins of the world,
Have mercy on us.

Lamb of God, you take away the sins of the world,
Have mercy on us.

Lamb of God, you take away the sins of the world,
Grant us peace.

O Christ, hear us.
O Christ, hear us.

Lord, have mercy upon us.
Christ, have mercy upon us.
Lord, have mercy upon us.

When the Litany is sung or said immediately before the Eucharist, the Litany concludes here, and the Eucharist begins with the Salutation and the Collect of the Day.

Bruce Jenneker

Prayers for the Lighting of Advent Candles

I.   Come, O Holy One, as the morning light after a wakeful night!
Keep us mindful that at any moment you may ask of us
an accounting of our lives;
help us to love you and love one another in all we do,
and so clothe us with your light
that we may bring others to love you also;
through Jesus our Savior. *Amen.*

II.   Come, O Holy One, as the water of life and refiner's fire!
Strengthen us with courage for your work of justice
that in all the creation and among every people
your peace may be established
and your joy abound;
through Jesus our Deliverer. *Amen.*

III.   Come, O Holy One, breaker of chains and renewer of life!
Open our eyes to your presence in all the earth.
Stir us to proclaim gladly the signs of your love:
the liberation of those oppressed,
the healing of those frail and broken,
springs of water in all the parched places,
and Jesus Christ risen and alive, through whom we pray.
Amen.

IV.   Come, O Holy One, as the beloved child, Emmanuel!
Soften our hearts and open our arms for your coming
that we may make this a place worthy and warm,
kindly and safe for all your children;
in the name of Jesus. *Amen.*

Jennifer Phillips

CHRISTMAS

PRAYER FOR THE OPENING OF GIFTS

Glory to you, Giver of all good gifts!
We offer you glad thanks and praise
for every blessing from your love,
and especially for the best gift of yourself
in the child Jesus. *Amen.*

Jennifer Phillips

CHRISTMAS CANDLE PRAYER

Welcome, Christ-Light, long awaited and desired one!
Give us the courage of your presence
to transform this world into a place fit for your arrival,
decked with justice, loving-kindness, and mercy,
glad with our songs of praise in company with the angels,
alive with your Holy Spirit. *Amen.*

Jennifer Phillips

EPIPHANY

FOR THE BLESSING OF WATER [AND SALT FOR A STOUP]
—adapted from The Book of Common Prayer 1979

Presider   The Lord be with you.
People   And also with you.
Presider   Let us pray.

It is desirable that water be poured audibly from a ewer into a basin on the altar during this prayer. A small dish of salt may also be placed on the altar. At "*" the salt is poured into the basin of water in the shape of a cross. At "+" the sign of the cross is made over the water.

We thank you, Most Holy God, for the gift of water. Over it the Holy Spirit moved in the beginning of creation. Through it you led the children of Israel out of their bondage in Egypt into the land of promise. In it your Son Jesus received the baptism of John and was anointed by the Holy Spirit as the Messiah, the Christ, to lead us through his death and resurrection, from the bondage of sin into everlasting life.

We thank you, Blessed One, for the water of baptism. In it we are buried with Christ in his death. By it we share in his resurrection. Through it we are reborn by the Holy Spirit.

[We thank you also, most merciful God, for the gift of salt. You commanded the prophet Elisha to cast salt into water to make it wholesome and clean. * Hallow this creature of salt for the casting out of all that is evil or unclean.]

Grant that by your power + those touched by this water as a reminder of their baptism may continue for ever in the risen life of Jesus Christ our Savior, to whom with you and the Holy Spirit we give honor and glory, now and for ever. *Amen.*

Jennifer Phillips

LENT

FIVE LENTEN PRAYERS

Lent 1

God, whose hands have molded all the earth;
bring us to the place of discernment
that we may never mistake the tinsel of the world
for your glory,
nor bow to that which is evil,
nor offer stones to those who hunger for bread,
but rather, serve you with a Sabbath mind
and worship you only;
through Jesus Christ, your Word near us. *Amen.*

Lent 2

God of generative joy,
replenish us in barren times,
lead us out of our habits of captivity
and into your country of promise;
in trouble, in emptiness of life, in sorrow,
let us never be separated from you,
that we may build in the wilderness an altar
and offer our whole hearts
to your renewing fire
and delivering mercy;
through Jesus Christ who gave himself for us. *Amen.*

Lent 3

God, whose unpronounceable name is Life:
when your people were a barren tree
you fed and watered us;
when we wandered in fear
you led us by fire and promise and your law;
when we gave ourselves up to corruption,
you drove evil out of us and raised us up
through your Anointed One, Jesus,
our Rock and Salvation;
through whom we give you praise! *Amen.*

Lent 4

God, by your love our eyes are opened,
our hunger fed, our sin forgiven,
and our wickedness overthrown;
may we so celebrate your blessing
as ambassadors of your gladness
that by our hands
the fragments of community may be gathered
and the lost welcomed home;
through Jesus our Reconciler. *Amen.*

Lent 5

Living God, you break into our mortal loneliness
by your coming among us.
You clothe the dry bones of our lives
with the flesh of your new creation,
and from our fearful tombs
you call us to come out and live unbound;
through the power of Christ's resurrection,
in whose strong name we give thanks. *Amen.*

Jennifer Phillips

EASTER

EUCHARISTIC PRAYER:
NEW LIFE, THE LORD, THE SPIRIT

—*adapted from Eucharistic Prayer IV,
The Scottish Liturgy 1982*

In this prayer, the lines in italics are spoken by the People.

The Celebrant faces them and sings or says

The Lord be with you.
And also with you.

Lift up your hearts.
We lift them to the Lord.

Let us give thanks to the Lord our God.
It is right to give our thanks and praise.

Splendor and honor are yours by right,
God of all being, your power sustains,
your endless love restores this broken world.
Always present with us,
you bring order out of chaos,
you fill our emptiness with life.

Christ, raised from the dead,
brings the dawn of hope.
His life in us
leads us to walk in your light.

Your Holy Spirit is fire in us,
your breath is power to purge our sin
and warm our hearts to love.

Children of your redeeming purpose,
freed when Christ burst from the tomb,
we offer you our praise
with Angels and Archangels,
and all the company of heaven,
singing your eternal glory:

Celebrant and People

Holy, holy, holy Lord, God of power and might,
heaven and earth are full of your glory.
Hosanna in the highest.
Blessed is the one who comes in the name of the Lord.
Hosanna in the highest.

The Celebrant continues

All praise is yours, Savior of the world,
for by your cross eternal life is ours
and death is swallowed up in victory.

On the night before Jesus was given up to death,
knowing that his hour had come,
and having loved his own,
he loved them to the end.
At supper with the disciples
Jesus took bread, offered thanks to you,
broke it, gave it to his friends and said:
"Take, eat, this is my Body given for you."

After supper, he took the cup,
offered thanks, gave it to them and said:
"This is my Blood of the new Covenant
poured out for you, and for all,
that sins may be forgiven.
Do this in remembrance of me."

In the first light of Easter,
glory broke from the tomb;
the women's sorrow changed to joy.
In the garden Mary found the truth;
the One whom they had loved and lost
was restored to them in every place and for ever.

So Christ renewed the promise of his presence:
known in the breaking of the bread,
bringing peace to fearful disciples.
The risen Christ proclaimed new birth in the Spirit
and consecrated your people to freedom.

And so we come, in obedience to Christ's command,
to proclaim the mystery of faith:

The Celebrant and People

Christ has died,
Christ is risen,
Christ will come again.

The Celebrant continues

One in Christ, we offer you these gifts,
and with them ourselves,
a holy, living sacrifice.

Hear us, merciful God:
send your Holy Spirit on us
and on this bread and wine
that they may be the Body and Blood of Christ;
kindle in us the fire of your love,
renew us for the service of your kingdom.

Help us live and work to your praise and glory;
that we may grow together in unity and love
until, at last, in your new creation,
we enter into the company of the Virgin Mary,
the apostles and prophets [especially _____],
and of all our sisters and brothers, the living and the dead;
through Jesus Christ our risen Savior
by whom, with whom, and in whom
in the unity of the Holy Spirit,
all honor and glory are yours
throughout all ages, now and for ever. *AMEN.*

Gregory Howe

Corpus Christi

A Pilgrimage of Prayer for Healing the Body of Christ

—written for use in St. Louis, Missouri, at the sites of murders in that community

At the corner of Enright and Aubert we remember Jevon Washington, 15, who died on April 3ʳᵈ.

Presider	Most Holy God, we commend to your mercy Jevon Washington. Rest eternal grant to him, O Lord; and let light perpetual shine upon him.
People	May his soul and the souls of all the departed through your mercy rest in peace. *Amen.*

The First Reading

O God,
We remember not only our son but also his murderers;
Not because they killed him in the prime of his youth
    and made our hearts bleed and our tears flow;
Not because with this savage act they have brought
    further disgrace upon the name of our country
    among the civilized nations of the world;
But because through their crime we now follow your footsteps
    more closely in the way of sacrifice.
The terrible fire of this calamity burns up all selfishness
    and possessiveness in us;
Its flame reveals the depth of depravity and meanness and suspicion,
    the dimension of hatred, and the measure of sinfulness in
    human nature;
It makes obvious as never before our need to trust in God's love
    as shown on the cross of Jesus and his resurrection;
Love which makes us free from hate toward our persecutors;
Love which brings patience, forbearance, courage, loyalty,
    humility, generosity, greatness of heart;
Love which more than ever deepens our trust in God's final victory
    and God's eternal designs for the Church and for the world;
Love which teaches us how to prepare ourselves to face our own
    day of death.

O God,
Our son's blood has multiplied the fruit of the Spirit in the soil of
   our souls;
So when his murderers stand before you on the day of judgment
Remember the fruit of the Spirit by which they have enriched
   our lives.
And forgive.

—*"A Father's Prayer Upon the Murder of His Son," Bishop Dehqani-Tafti of Iran in
Guide My Feet: Prayers and Meditaions for Our Children, Marian Wright Edelman*

*On the corner of McMillan and Walton we remember William Davis, 35, who
died on January 25th.*

Presider	Most Holy God, we commend to your mercy William Davis. Rest eternal grant to him, O Lord; and let light perpetual shine upon him.
People	May his soul and the souls of all the departed through your mercy rest in peace. Amen.

Second Reading

Reader and People

O God, hold and heal the anger of the world today.

The Reader continues

Today, Holy One, let one person turn and walk away from a fight;
Today, let one bullet go wide of its mark
      and one young man with a gun be horrified at the death
      he nearly caused and lay it down.
Today, let one mother in the emergency room
      awaiting the death of her child hear good news of life saved.
Today, let one father come home after a long absence to embrace
   his teenager.

The People respond

O God, hold and heal the anger of the world today.

The Reader continues

Today, Holy One, let one city block get together to plan for the
   safety of their children.
Today, let one legislator shoot some hoops with a group of boys
   without hope, and come home with a changed heart.

Today, let one more bomb be dismantled than is built,
      and one more mine defused than is laid in the ground.
Today, let the diplomats of two warring nations find a first point
      of agreement and believe in the possibility of peace.

The People respond

O God, hold and heal the anger of the world today.

The Reader continues

Today, Holy One, let two families on opposite sides of a war
      come together to celebrate the marriage of their children.
Today, let the last ember of an old resentment burn out.
Today, let a little child of the city lean his back against a tree and
      feel safe and content.
Today, let even my anger dissolve into grief and breathe itself out
      into quietness.

The People respond

O God, hold and heal the anger of the world today.
                —*Jennifer Phillips, Trinity Parish, St. Louis, 1996*

And a few doors along the 4700 block of Kensington Place, we remember Damon Norris, 20, who died on February 9th.

Presider	Most Holy God, we commend to your mercy Damon Norris. Rest eternal grant to him, O Lord; and let light perpetual shine upon him.
People	May his soul and the souls of all the departed through your mercy rest in peace. *Amen.*

Third Reading

O Thou light of the world, shine in upon our darkness and illumine the truth that all people may see it. For human beings are more ignorant than wicked—willfully ignorant it is true and wickedly willful—and yet it is because the world does not know and realize the truth about itself and about its human children that it is continually doing such monstrous and hurtful things. Give us then light, more light, O God, that we may see and learn and know and we may no longer be with them that sit in darkness. Amen.
                —*W.E.B. Du Bois, Prayers for a Dark People*

At the corner of McMillan and Taylor we remember Roland Martin, 40, who died March 29th.

Presider	Most Holy God, we commend to your mercy Roland Martin. Rest eternal grant to him, O Lord; and let light perpetual shine upon him.
People	May his soul and the souls of all the departed through your mercy rest in peace. *Amen.*

Fourth Reading

A Reader begins the fourth reading.

The lines in italics are the responses of the People.

We are called to proclaim the truth. . . . And let us believe:
It is not true that this world and its people are doomed to die and to be lost.
This is true: I have come that they might have life in all its abundance.

It is not true that we must accept inhumanity and discrimination, hunger and poverty, death and destruction.
This is true: the deaf hear, the dead are raised to life, the poor are hearing the good news.

It is not true that violence and hatred should have the last word, and that war and destruction have come to stay for ever.
This is true: death shall be no more, neither shall there be mourning nor crying nor pain any more.

It is not true that we are simply victims of the powers of evil who seek to rule the world.
This is true: the Lord whom we seek will suddenly come to God's temple; the One who is like a refiner's fire.

It is not true that our dreams of liberation, of human dignity, are not meant for this earth and for this history.
This is true: it is already time for us to wake from sleep. For the night is far gone, the day is at hand.

—from a 1983 World Council of Churches address by
Allan Boesak of South Africa

On the corner of Taylor and Enright, we remember Carlos Bell, 22, who died March 28th.

Presider	Most Holy God, we commend to your mercy Carlos Bell. Rest eternal grant to him, O Lord; and let light perpetual shine upon him.
People	May his soul and the souls of all the departed through your mercy rest in peace. *Amen.*

Fifth Reading

A Reader begins the fifth reading.

The lines in italics are the responses of the People.

The Word, for our sake, became poverty clothed as the poor who live off the refuse heap.
The Word, for our sake, became a sob a thousand times stifled in the immovable mouth of the child who died from hunger.

The Word, for our sake, became danger in the anguish of the mother who worries about her son growing into manhood.
The Word cut us deeply in that place of shame: the painful reality of the poor.

The Word blew its spirit over the dried bones of the churches, guardians of silence.
The Word awoke us from the lethargy which had robbed us of our hope.

The Word became a path in the jungle, a decision on the farm, love among people, unity among workers, and a Star for those few who can inspire dreams.
The Word became Light. The Word became History. The Word became Conflict.

The Word became indomitable Spirit, and sowed its seeds upon the mountain, near the river and in the valley,
And those of good will heard the angels sing.

Tired knees were strengthened, trembling hands were stilled, and the people who wandered in darkness saw the light.
The Word became the seed of justice and we conceived peace. The Word made justice to rain and peace came forth from the furrows in the land. And we saw its glory in the eyes of the poor transformed into real men and women.

And those who saw the Star opened for us the path we now follow.
The Word became flesh!

—adapted from Julia Esquivel of Guatemala

On the corner of Delmar and Walton, we remember Corey Holland, 24, who died March 12th.

Presider	Most Holy God, we commend to your mercy Corey Holland. Rest eternal grant to him, O Lord; and let light perpetual shine upon him.
People	May his soul and the souls of all the departed through your mercy rest in peace. *Amen.*

Sixth Reading

Lord, you placed us in the world
to be its salt.
We were afraid of committing ourselves,
afraid of being stained by the world.
We did not want to hear what 'they' might say.
And our salt dissolved as if in water.

Forgive us, Jesus.
Lord, you placed us in the world
to be its light.
We were afraid of the shadows,
afraid of the poverty.
We did not want to know other people.
And our light slowly faded away.
Forgive us, Jesus.

Lord, you placed us in the world
to live in community.
Thus you taught us to love,
to share in life,
to struggle for bread and for justice,
your truth incarnate in our lives.
So be it, Jesus.

—adapted from Peggy M. deCueblo of Uruguay, Your Will Be Done

At the parish's front door

Seventh Reading

A Reader begins the seventh reading.

The lines in italics are the responses of the People.

O God, the source of our common life,
when we are dry and scattered,
when we are divided and alone,
we long for connection, we long for community.
Breath of God, breathe on us.

With those we live beside,
who are often strange to us,
whom we are afraid to approach,
yet who have riches of friendship to share,
we long for connection, we long for community.
Breath of God, breathe on us.

With those we have only heard of,
who see with different eyes,
whose struggles we try to imagine,
whose fierce joy we wish we could grasp,
we long for connection, we long for community.
Breath of God, breathe on us.

With those whose lives we shall never know,
but whose lives are linked with ours,
whose shared ground we stand on,
and whose common air we breathe,
we long for connection, we long for community.
Breath of God, breathe on us.

When we are dry and scattered,
when we are divided and alone,
when we are cut off from the source of our life,
open our graves, O God,
that all your people may be free to breathe, strong to move,
and joyful to stand together
to celebrate your name. *Amen.*

—*Janet Morley, Christian Aid 1990, Bread of Tomorrow*

In the church, the people enter the pews and remain standing.

Presider

Give us, O God, the gift of human charity. Lead us to know that, bad as human nature is and dark as our passion may be, most people are always a little better than the worst, always more decent than our rash judgment tries to paint. Give us the humility to realize that few of us put in their places—with their hurts and hindrances and their vision of right—few of us would do better than they, and many would do far worse. Perhaps God meant just this when he said: *Blessed* are the meek. *Amen.*

—W.E.B. Du Bois, *Prayers for a Dark People*

O God, who wonderfully created, and yet more wonderfully restored, the dignity of human nature: Grant that we may share the divine life of him who humbled himself to share our humanity, your Son Jesus Christ; who lives and reigns with you, in the unity of the Holy Spirit, one God, for ever and ever. *Amen.*

—from *The Book of Common Prayer*, p. 214

Benediction follows an interval of silent prayer. The people leave the service quietly.

Jennifer Phillips

NOTES

First Reading:

The Rt. Rev. Hassan Barnaba Dehqani-Tafti, Bishop of Iran, Jurisdiction of the Archbishop in Jerusalem, "A Father's Prayer Upon the Murder of His Son," in *Guide My Feet: Prayers and Meditations for Our Children*, Marian Wright Edelman (Boston: Beacon Press, 1995).

Third Reading:

W.E.B. Du Bois, *Prayers for a Dark People* (Amherst: University of Massachusetts, 1980), p. 32.

Fifth Reading:

adapted from Julia Esquivel, Guatemala, *Threatened with Resurrection* (Elgin IL: Brethren Press, 1982).

Sixth Reading:
> adapted from Peggy M. deCuehlo, Uruguay, *Your Will Be Done* (Christian Conference of Asia Youth, 1984).

Seventh Reading:
> Janet Morley, Christian Aid 1990, *Bread of Tomorrow* (London: SPCK, 1992).

First Closing Prayer:
> W.E.B. Du Bois, *Prayers for a Dark People*, p. 24.

Second Closing Prayer:
> The Book of Common Prayer, "Collects: Contemporary," p. 214.

A LITANY OF THE BLESSED SACRAMENT

The Litanist begins and the People respond.

O God, the Father of heaven,
Have mercy on us.

O God the Son, Redeemer of the world,
Have mercy on us.

O God the Holy Spirit,
Have mercy on us.

Holy Trinity, one God,
Have mercy on us.

Bread of angels,
Have mercy on us.

Bread meet to be our food,
Have mercy on us.

Bread most fair and royal feast,
Have mercy on us.

Living Bread that came down from heaven,
Have mercy on us.

Bread to strengthen our hearts,
Have mercy on us.

Corn of God's chosen people,
Have mercy on us.

Hidden manna,
Have mercy on us.

Spiritual refreshment,
Have mercy on us.

Purest feast,
Have mercy on us.

Our food and our Guest,
Have mercy on us.

Remedy to preserve us from death,
Have mercy on us.

Memorial of God's marvelous acts,
Have mercy on us.

Wondrous among all miracles,
Have mercy on us.

Victim most holy,
Have mercy on us.

Cup of blessing,
Have mercy on us.

Offering most pure,
Have mercy on us.

Sacrifice that abides,
Have mercy on us.

Broken bread made one,
Have mercy on us.

Sweetest banquet,
Have mercy on us.

Mystery of faith,
Have mercy on us.

Bond of charity,
Have mercy on us.

Refreshment of holy souls,
Have mercy on us.

Last food of those that die in the Lord,
Have mercy on us.

Pledge of glory yet to be,
Have mercy on us.

Sacrament of mercy,
Have mercy on us.

Sacrament that gives life,
Have mercy on us.

Worthy of revering,
Have mercy on us.

Hidden God,
Have mercy on us.

Word made flesh,
Have mercy on us.

From all disorder of the flesh,
Deliver us, O Lord.

From all pride of life,
Deliver us, O Lord.

From all sin,
Deliver us, O Lord.

From all works of evil,
Deliver us, O Lord.

By the desire with which you desired to eat this Passover
        with the disciples,
Deliver us, O Lord.

By the deep humility with which you washed the disciples' feet,
Deliver us, O Lord.

By the burning love with which you instituted this holy Sacrament,
Deliver us, O Lord.

By your precious blood, shed upon the cross for us,
Deliver us, O Lord.

By your rising from the tomb,
Deliver us, O Lord.

We sinners
Beseech you to hear us.

We children of the most high
Beseech you to hear us.

That it may please you to increase and preserve in us faith
        and reverence for this blessed Sacrament,
We beseech you to hear us.

That you may stir up in us a burning desire of receiving you
        in this heavenly bread,
We beseech you to hear us.

That you may impart to us the fruits of this life-giving Sacrament,
We beseech you to hear us.

That you may strengthen us for service by this gracious meal,
We beseech you to hear us.

That you may strengthen and fortify us at the hour of our death
     with this bread for the journey,
We beseech you to hear us.

That we may have a foretaste of the banquet table
     where you are Host,
We beseech you to hear us.

Lord, have mercy,
Christ, have mercy.
Lord, have mercy.

O God, who comes to us in this wonderful Sacrament: grant us so to venerate the sacred mysteries of your Body and Blood and to be transformed by them, that we may ever perceive within ourselves the fruit of your redemption; who lives and reigns one holy and undivided Trinity, world without end. *Amen.*

Jennifer Phillips

ALL SAINTS' DAY

A LITANY OF SAINTS

The Litanist begins and the People respond.

Holy God, Creator of heaven and earth,
Have mercy on us.

Holy and Mighty, Redeemer of the world,
Have mercy on us.

Holy Immortal One, Sanctifier of the faithful,
Have mercy on us.

Holy, blessed, and glorious Trinity, One God,
Have mercy on us.

Surrounded by the great cloud of witnesses to the Love of God incarnate in Jesus Christ,
We are strengthened for the journey.

In the company of Mary, the Mother of Jesus, and Joseph, her spouse and protector,
We are strengthened for the journey.

In the company of angels, archangels, and all the creatures who sing God's praises,
We are strengthened for the journey.

In the company of Matthew, Mark, Luke, John, and all who tell the Gospel story,
We are strengthened for the journey.

In the company of Mary Magdalene, Martha and Mary of Bethany, and all the women who follow and care for Jesus,
We are strengthened for the journey.

In the company of innocent children slain by Pharaoh, Herod, Hitler, and other tyrants through the ages,
We are strengthened for the journey.

In the company of Stephen, first martyr; Alban, first martyr of Britain; Perpetua and Felicity, martyred while nursing their infants; and all who die for the faith we proclaim,
We are strengthened for the journey.

In the company of Benedict and Scholastica and all monastic women and men who desire God above all else,
We are strengthened for the journey.

In the company of Clare and Francis, who relinquished material wealth to preach the riches of God's realm for all,
We are strengthened for the journey.

In the company of Mother Teresa, William Wilberforce, and all who care for the suffering and the oppressed,
We are strengthened for the journey.

In the company of all who heal body, mind, and spirit through prayer, counsel, medication, therapies, and love,
We are strengthened for the journey.

In the company of holy teachers who lead us to deeper knowledge of God and the ways of righteousness and peace,
We are strengthened for the journey.

In the company of all the baptized and all who seek to do God's work of peace and justice,
We are strengthened for the journey.

Holy God,
Make us holy.

Self-giving God,
Make us generous.

Loving God,
Make us loving.

Wisdom of God,
Dwell in us.

Patience of God,
Keep us steadfast in faith and work.

Holy One, we, too, would serve you as your saints. Strengthen our wills, help us to grow in love and knowledge of you, and to speak your Word through our words and actions. We pray in Jesus' name. *Amen.*

Elizabeth Morris Downie

Collect for All Hallows'

O God, our shield and our armor of light, whom we adore with all the angelic host: defend us from evil; watch over any who are in danger this night and give your angels charge over them; and grant that we may always rejoice in your heavenly protection and serve you faithfully and bravely in the world; through Jesus Christ our Savior. *Amen.*

Jennifer Phillips

THE CALENDAR
OF SAINTS

January 9: Julia Chester Emery
July 19: Macrina
July 20: Elizabeth Cady Stanton, Amelia Bloomer, Sojourner Truth, Harriet Ross Tubman
September 9: Constance and Her Companions
September 17: Hildegard of Bingen

LITANY OF WOMEN'S MINISTRIES

*—written for Holy Eucharist, celebrating the ministry of women,
General Convention of the Episcopal Church, August 28, 1994*

Leader   Let us remember before God and one another the
sacred story of women in the Episcopal Church, saying,
"We remember."
Women who remain steadfast in the faith, bearing witness to
God's love:
Pocahontas, one of the first Native Americans converted to the
Anglican Church;
Native American women and African-American slave women
converted to the Christian faith during the colonial period and the
expansion of the United States;
Elizabeth Cady Stanton, Amelia Bloomer, Sojourner Truth,
and Harriet Ross Tubman, liberators and prophets;
women evangelists, who proclaimed the Good News.

The People may name other individuals.

Leader   God of our sacred story,
People   We remember.

The Leader continues

Women whose teaching helps us grow in the knowledge and love
of God:
Macrina, monastic and teacher;
Hildegard, Abbess of Bingen, and mystic;
Anne Wager, teacher in a colonial missionary school for
African-American children;
women teachers in Freedom Schools after the Civil War;
Susan Knapp, Dean of the New York Training School for
Deaconesses;
women who taught in schools for deaconesses;

women serving on seminary faculties;
women serving as parish Directors of Religious Education;
women teaching in Sunday Schools.

The People may name other individuals.

Leader God of our sacred story,
People We remember.

The Leader continues

Women missionaries, deaconesses, and members of the Church Army, serving in this country and abroad:
 Frances Hill and Mrs. J.J. Robertson, first women overseas missionaries;
 deaconesses who served in the nineteenth century without official recognition by the Church;
 women officially set apart as deaconesses, beginning in 1892.

The People may name other individuals.

Leader God of our sacred story,
People We remember.

The Leader continues

Founders and members of Episcopal religious orders for women:
 Anne Ayres, founder of the Sisterhood of the Holy Communion;
 Harriet Starr Cannon, founder of the Community of Saint Mary.
The People may name other individuals.

Leader God of our sacred story,
People We remember.

The Leader continues

Members and leaders of Episcopal women's organizations:
 Mary Abbott Emery and Julia Chester Emery, founders of the Woman's Auxiliary to the Board of Missions;
 Ida Soule, founder of the United Thank Offering;
 Mattie Hopkins, spiritual mother, and Gloria Brown, Edna Brown, Judith Conley, Carmen Guerrero, Margaret Hardy, and Carol Jan Lee, founding members of ABIL—Asian, Black, Indian/Indigenous, and Latina women of the Episcopal Church.

The People may name other individuals.

Leader	God of our sacred story,
People	We remember.

The Leader continues

Women serving on the councils of the Church, in parish, diocese, province, and national Church:

Elizabeth Dyer, seated as General Convention Deputy in 1946;

women Deputies—Alice H. Cowdry, Elizabeth Davis Pittman, Ruth Jenkins, Mrs. Domingo Villafane—denied voice and vote at the 1949 General Convention;

women seated as Deputies after the 1970 General Convention which removed constitutional barriers to the seating of women;

Pamela P. Chinnis, first woman to be President of the House of Deputies.

The People may name other individuals.

Leader	God of our sacred story,
People	We remember.

The Leader continues

Women and men who labored for the full participation of women in the decision-making bodies of the Episcopal Church.

The People may name individuals.

Leader	God of our sacred story,
People	We remember.

The Leader continues

Women ordained or recognized as deacons after the 1970 General Convention.

The People may name individuals.

Leader	God of our sacred story,
People	We remember.

The Leader continues

Women who serve as priests in the Church:

women ordained to the priesthood in Philadelphia in 1974—Merrill Bittner, Alla Bozarth-Campbell, Allison Cheek, Emily Hewitt, Carter Heyward, Suzanne Hiatt, Marie Moorefield, Jeannette Piccard, Betty Bone Schiess, Katrina Welles Swanson, Nancy

Hatch Wittig—and in Washington in 1975—E. Lee McGee, Alison Palmer, Elizabeth Rosenberg, Diane Tickell;
women ordained to the priesthood in 1977 after General Convention approved the ordination of women.

The People may name individuals.

Leader	God of our sacred story,
People	We remember.

The Leader continues

The first women bishops in the Episcopal Church:
Barbara Clementine Harris, Jane Holmes Dixon, Mary Adelia McLeod.

Leader	God of our sacred story,
People	We remember.

The Leader continues

Women and men who labored for the full inclusion of women in all orders of ministry in the Episcopal Church; for the Episcopal Women's Caucus.

The People may name individuals.

Leader	God of our sacred story,
People	We remember.

The Leader continues

Let us give thanks to God for the diversity of women's ministries, saying, "We give you thanks."
For women who work for justice and peace;
women who offer themselves in charity and service to those in need;
women of prophetic vision and action.

The People may name individuals.

Leader	God of abundant blessing,
People	We give you thanks.

The Leader continues

For women who enrich the Church and the world with their intellectual gifts:
> women who serve in government and business;
> women who cultivate the earth and women who protect its resources.

The People may name individuals.

Leader	God of abundant blessing,
People	We give you thanks.

The Leader continues

For women who offer hospitality and nurture:
> women artisans, writers, musicians, and other artists, creators of beauty;
> women of spiritual wisdom and women ministers of healing.

The People may name individuals.

Leader	God of abundant blessing,
People	We give you thanks.

The Leader continues

For women as mother; women who sustain the life of the Church by quiet acts of service:
> on the Altar Guild; in the kitchen;
> in nurseries and nursing homes;
> in classrooms, meeting rooms, and offices.

The People may name individuals.

Leader	God of abundant blessing,
People	We give you thanks.

The Leader continues

> Let us acknowledge our sins against God, one another, and ourselves, saying "Forgive us."

For our disregard for the dignity of every human being; and especially for our prejudices against women who have disabilities or whose racial identity or sexual orientation is different from our own,

Leader   God of infinite mercy,
People   Forgive us.

The Leader continues

For the subordination of women and the Church's complicity in that subordination,

Leader   God of infinite mercy,
People   Forgive us.

The Leader continues

For our stubborn clinging to old forms and our unwillingness to grow and change in response to your call,

Leader   God of infinite mercy,
People   Forgive us.

The Leader continues

For all our sins, known and unknown, things done and left undone,

Leader   God of infinite mercy,
People   Forgive us.

The Leader continues

Let us offer our prayers for the Church and the world, saying, "Receive our prayer."
For the holy people of God throughout the world, for the Episcopal Church and its leaders, lay and ordained, and for this General Convention,

Leader   God of grace and wisdom,
People   Receive our prayer.

The Leader continues

For justice and peace among the nations and peoples of the world, for the leaders of the nations, and for all in positions of public trust,

The People may add their own petitions.

Leader   God of righteousness,
People   Receive our prayer.

The Leader continues

For those in any need or affliction: the hungry and the homeless, the destitute and the oppressed, those who are sick or wounded, prisoners and captives, victims of war and civil strife,

The People may add their own petitions.

Leader God of compassion,
People Receive our prayer.

The Leader continues

For all who have died,

The People may add their own petitions.

Leader God of eternal life,
People Receive our prayer.

Celebrant

Gracious God, source of life and giver of all good gifts, we thank you for the women who have ministered in your name throughout the ages. Grant us courage and compassion, that we may stand as daughters and sons of these women, ever receptive to your grace and faithful to your call. All this we ask in the name of Jesus Christ, our Savior and Redeemer. *Amen.*

Ruth A. Meyers

March 1: David of Wales

Eucharistic Prayer

—after the Celtic tradition

In this prayer, the lines in italics are spoken by the People.

The Celebrant faces them and sings or says

The Lord be with you.
And also with you.

Lift up your hearts.
We lift them to the Lord.

Let us give thanks to God.
It is right to give our thanks and praise.

We give thanks and praise to you, O God the One in Three:
One in wisdom as you created all that is,
One in goodness as you spoke the word of life to your creatures,
One in blessing as you saved us from sin, evil, and death;

That we have failed to love you as we ought,
we acknowledge; Good Judge, pardon us;
that we have not served your people,
we confess; Good Shepherd, have mercy on us;
that we do not resist evil,
we repent; Good Savior, deliver us.

We bless you for strengthening us by the witness of our ancestors:
by the blood of martyrs, the constancy of exiles, the fortitude
        of prophets,
the holiness of life of those who have gone before us;

We bless you for giving blessed David [blessed N.], and all the saints
as our companions at work and at table;
With them and with the joyful hosts of heaven we sing (say):

Celebrant and People

Holy, holy, holy! God of power and might,
heaven and earth are full of your glory.
Hosanna in the highest.
Blessed is the one who comes in the name of our God.
Hosanna in the highest.

The Celebrant continues

We bless you, God, for armoring us with light for the work of justice
and for encircling us with your constant love;
bless to us all our actions and desires,
all our learnings, and the yearnings of our hearts.

And above all, we bless you for blessing us
through your child Jesus, born of Mary our sister, and the Holy Spirit;
for sanctifying our bodies and our lives through Jesus Christ,
who sat at supper with his friends and took bread,
blessed, broke, and gave it to them all saying,
"Take, eat: This is my Body which is given for you.
Do this for the remembrance of me."

After supper, Jesus took the cup of wine and said,
"Drink this all of you: This is my Blood of the new Covenant
poured out for you and for all for the forgiveness of sin.
Whenever you drink it, do this for the remembrance of me."

Therefore we affirm in Jesus:

Celebrant and People

Your love faithful even to death,
Your power which raised Christ to life,
Your promise that Christ will come in glory!

The Celebrant continues

And we lift up to you, along with all our lives,
these gifts of bread and wine.
Send the fire of your Spirit upon them
that they may be for us the very Body and Blood of Christ;
enkindle us also with the light of your Spirit

that we may show you forth to all the world,
that every corner of creation may be filled
with the radiance of your delight and design.

Send us forth, in the name of the Three,
in the company of the saints,
in the enfolding of the One,
to serve your people and offer you praise,
by, with, and in Jesus Christ our Savior,
today and always. *AMEN.*

Jennifer Phillips

APRIL 21: ANSELM OF CANTERBURY

EUCHARISTIC PRAYER

—from the writings of Anselm of Canterbury

In this prayer, the lines in italics are spoken by the People.

The Celebrant faces them and sings or says

God be with you.
And also with you.

Lift up your hearts.
We lift them to the Holy One.

Let us give thanks to God.
It is right to give our thanks and praise.

We thank you, God, that by your wisdom you created us
and all things of your goodness
and though we repaid so poorly the riches of your love,
you did not give us over to our ignorance and weakness,
but sent Jesus Christ to be born of our sister Mary by the Holy Spirit,
assuming human nature, not to hide yourself in flesh,
but to reveal what was not yet known of your love.

Jesus our mother,
longing to bear your children into life, you tasted death
and by your dying birthed us.
When we were destitute of all help, you illuminated us
and showed us what we were, before we asked.
You set us upright
and raised us to the knowledge and love of yourself.
We owe you all our being; you draw us to you in the fullness of love;
we who are wholly yours by creation,
make us all yours, too, in love, completely held in your care.

All of heaven, stars, earth, waters, day, and night, rejoice now
for the new and splendid grace given them through Christ,
for all things were as if dead, buried by oppression, and tainted
        by false use,
but now are raised in life to praise God;

hell itself is redeemed, powers of evil trampled down,
and we are saved.
So with the company of heaven and all creation we sing (say):

Celebrant and People

Holy, holy, holy! God of power and might,
heaven and earth are full of your glory.
Hosanna in the highest.
Blessed is the one who comes in the name of our God.
Hosanna in the highest!

The Celebrant continues

We thank you that on the night before he died for us,
our Savior Jesus Christ took bread,
and when he had given thanks to you, he broke it,
gave it to his friends, and said,
"Take, eat: This is my Body given for you.
Do this for the remembrance of me."

When supper was ending, Jesus took the cup of wine,
again gave thanks to you, and said,
"This is my Blood of the new Covenant
which is shed for you and for all for the forgiveness of sin.
Whenever you drink it, do this for the remembrance of me."

Grant that this bread and wine may be,
by the power of your Holy Spirit
for us the very Body and Blood of Jesus Christ,
our Redeemer, our Mercy, and our Salvation.

So much as we can, though not as much as we ought:

Celebrant and People

we are mindful of your passion, death, and burial,
we remember your glorious Resurrection and Ascension,
holding all this with unwavering faith
and hoping for the consolation of your coming,
that we may see the joy that we desire!

The Celebrant continues

As we offer to you from your creation
this bread, this wine, and ourselves,
most kind Lord,
acknowledge what is yours in us,
and take away anything that is not yours.
Through the grace of this holy Sacrament
take us into the wide heart of your mercy,
that with blessed Anselm [blessed N.], and all the saints,
we may enjoy, praise, and glorify you,
being enkindled and stirred to justice by your love.
Hope of our hearts, strength of our souls,
by your powerful kindness complete
what we in our weakness only attempt,
and let our desire for you be as great
as our love ought to be,
until we enter into the joy of our Savior,
who is God, one and triune, blessed for ever. *AMEN.*

Jennifer Phillips

MAY 8: JULIAN OF NORWICH

EUCHARISTIC PRAYER

—from the writings of Julian of Norwich

In this prayer, the lines in italics are spoken by the People.

The Celebrant faces them and sings or says

The Lord be with you.
And also with you.

Lift up your hearts.
We lift them to the Lord.

Let us give thanks to the Lord our God.
It is right to give our thanks and praise.

It is right, and a good and joyful thing,
always and everywhere to give you thanks,
our great Father, almighty God.
You are being.
You know and love us from before time began.
Out of this knowledge,
in your most wonderful deep love,
by the eternal counsel of all the blessed Trinity,
you willed the second Person to become our Mother, our Brother,
    and our Savior.
As truly, therefore, as you, God, are our Father,
so truly are you our Mother.
Our Father, you will,
Our Mother, you work,
Our Lord the Holy Spirit, you confirm.
Therefore, it is our part to love you in whom we have our being,
reverently thanking and praising you for our creation.

And so we join the saints and angels in proclaiming your glory,
as we sing (say):

Celebrant and People

Holy, holy, holy Lord, God of power and might,
heaven and earth are full of your glory.
Hosanna in the highest.
Blessed is he who comes in the name of the Lord.
Hosanna in the highest.

The Celebrant continues

Truly holy, truly blessed are you, most loving God,
for when we have fallen, through frailty or blindness,
then, courteous Lord, you touch us, stir and call us.
You will that we should see our wretchedness and humbly
        acknowledge it.
But it is not your will that we should remain like this,
nor that we should busy ourselves too much with self-accusation;
nor is it your will that we should despise ourselves.
But you will that we should quickly turn to you,
like children, distressed and frightened,
who run quickly to our mother,
and unable to do more,
call to the mother for help with all our might.

So, like trusting children, we cry,
Beloved Mother, have mercy on us.
Give us your help and grace.
For Jesus, our heavenly Mother is almighty,
all wisdom and all love, and so is none but he,
blessed may he be.

For on the night before he died for us,
our Savior Jesus Christ took bread;
and when he had given thanks to you,
he broke it, and gave it to his friends, and said,
"Take, eat: This is my Body, which is given for you.
Do this for the remembrance of me."

As supper was ending, Jesus took the cup of wine;
and when he had given thanks,
he gave it to them, and said,
"Drink this, all of you: This is my Blood of the new Covenant,

which is poured out for you and for all for the forgiveness of sins.
Whenever you drink it,
do this for the remembrance of me."

Therefore we proclaim the mystery of faith:

Celebrant and People

Christ has died.
Christ is risen.
Christ will come again.

The Celebrant continues

Remembering now the suffering and death,
and proclaiming the resurrection and ascension
of Jesus our Redeemer,
we bring before you these gifts.
Sanctify them by your Holy Spirit
to be for your people the Body and Blood of Christ.
As a mother gives her child to suck of her milk,
so our precious Mother Jesus feeds us with himself,
most courteously and tenderly,
with the blessed sacrament,
which is the precious food of true life.
For you, O God, sustain us and all that is,
most mercifully and graciously,
though we are but as a hazelnut in your hand;
through Christ and with Christ and in Christ,
in the unity of the Holy Spirit,
to you be honor, glory, and praise,
for ever and ever. *AMEN.*

Paula S. D. Barker
Leonel L. Mitchell

OCTOBER 4: FRANCIS OF ASSISI

BLESSING OF ANIMALS
—written for Christ Church/Holy Cross in Dover, Delaware

*All stand and sing hymn #400, "All creatures of our God and King,"
from The Hymnal 1982.*

In the name of the holy and undivided Trinity. *Amen.*

May God, who is wonderful in all works, be with you all.
And also with you.

The animals of God's creation inhabit the skies, the earth, and the
sea. They share in the fortunes of human existence and have a part
in human life. God, who confers gifts on all living things, has often
used the service of animals or made them symbolic reminders of
the gifts of salvation. Animals were saved from the flood and
afterwards made a part of the covenant with Noah *(Genesis
9:9–10)*. The Paschal Lamb brings to mind the Passover Sacrifice
and the deliverance from the bondage of Egypt *(Exodus 12:3–14)*;
a giant fish saved Jonah *(Jonah 2:1–11)*; ravens brought bread to
Elijah *(1 Kings 17:6)*; animals were included in the repentance
enjoined on humans *(Jonah 3:7)*.

And animals share in Christ's redemption of all God's creation.

We therefore invoke the divine blessing on these animals through
the intercession of St. Francis. As we do so, let us praise the Creator and give thanks to God for setting us over other creatures of
the earth. Let us also pray that, remembering our dignity, we may
always walk in God's law.

O God,
You have done all things wisely; in your goodness you have made
us in your image and given us care over other living things. Grant
that these animals may serve our needs and that your bounty in
the resources of this life may move us to seek more confidently the
goal of eternal life. We ask this through Christ our Lord. *Amen.*

My brothers and sisters, listen to the words of the Book of Genesis:

> So out of the ground the Lord God formed every
> animal of the field and every bird of the air, and
> brought them to the man to see what he would call
> them; and whatever the man called every living
> creature, that was its name. The man gave names
> to all cattle, and to the birds of the air, and to every
> animal of the field.
>
> —*Genesis 2:19–20a*

Act of Commitment and Dedication

Gracious and everliving God, in praising you, we make our true worship. As Adam named the animals, you gave him stewardship over your creation. Help us to live faithfully with the friends we have brought here today, that our relationship to them may be a sign of our acceptance of your love and care for us.

People   Lord, I present _____ and I give you thanks for *her*. Help me to understand my responsibility for *her* as a pledge of my response to you for the love you show in Jesus Christ, and make me ever mindful of my responsibility, in his name, for all your creatures, great and small. Amen.

Prayer of Blessing of Animals

O God, the author and giver of every gift: animals also are part of the way you provide help for our needs and labors. We pray through the intercession of St. Francis that you will make available for our use the things we need to maintain a decent human life. We ask this through Christ our Redeemer. *Amen.*

Gregory Howe

FOUR SAINTS

NOVEMBER 16: MARGARET, QUEEN OF SCOTLAND, 1093

God of grace and mercy, you made Margaret a partner in the works of your loving-kindness. Give us a devotion like hers in your service, so that we may be agents of your justice, and true servants of your mercy; through Jesus our Redeemer, who is alive with you and the Holy Spirit, one God throughout all ages. *Amen.*

NOVEMBER 17: HUGH, BISHOP OF LINCOLN, 1200

God of peace, by your grace you made Hugh wise and faithful to stand boldly before sovereigns, and to serve his people with humility. Help us to share in your goodness, so that our worship may be leavened with your justice, and, fearing nothing but the loss of you, we may boldly speak the truth in love; through Jesus our Redeemer, who is alive with you and the Holy Spirit, one God, now and for ever. *Amen.*

NOVEMBER 18: HILDA, ABBESS OF WHITBY, 680

Eternal God, you girded Hilda with gifts of justice and holy strength, making her a judge among your people. Help us to instruct one another in the knowledge and love of your mercy, and so bring us closer to the heart of the holy and undivided Trinity, alive and life-giving throughout all ages. *Amen.*

NOVEMBER 19: ELIZABETH, PRINCESS OF HUNGARY, 1231

Loving God, your servant Elizabeth honored Jesus by ministering to the poor, making herself like them. Give us the grace to follow her example, that with gladness, we may devote ourselves to any we find in need or trouble, for the sake of your compassionate Christ. *Amen.*

Phoebe Pettingell

PASTORAL OCCASIONS

The Needs of the World

For Local Government

Grant, O God, that those who serve _____ may understand their office as a commission from you. May they bring to their deliberations minds informed by your wisdom, and hearts filled with compassion for your people. Give them a vision of your will, that they may never be enslaved by routine, convention, or pressure; but in all things let them be upheld by your free spirit to do justice, love mercy, and walk always in your paths. *Amen.*

Gregory Howe

For All Who Work for Public Safety

Versicle They shall call upon me and I will answer them.
Response I am with them in trouble; I will rescue them and bring them to honor.

O God, our strong tower and defense; guard all those who labor for the safety of your people: firefighters, law enforcement and security personnel, those who serve in the armed forces, and others who defend the peace of the city; hasten to their help in times of crisis; endue them with temperance and sound judgment; greet them in all those they serve; and keep them in safety; through Jesus Christ our Savior. *Amen.*

Jennifer Phillips

For the Homeless and Neglected

Versicle Those who dwell in the shadow of the most high
Response Abide under the shadow of the Almighty.

O God, defender of the poor, we remember before you all homeless and neglected persons, and those living in poverty and need. Rise up, O God, and maintain their cause; help us to share with one another as you have shared with us; for the love of your Son who for our sake became poor, Jesus Christ our Savior. *Amen.*

Jennifer Phillips

IN A TIME OF WAR

O God, governor and judge of all nations: we have lifted our hands to war, seeking what is right; yet, knowing our sin, we humbly pray you to bring a speedy end to bloodshed, and to serve in all our actions your eternal peace; through Jesus Christ our Savior. *Amen.*

Jennifer Phillips

Eucharistic Prayer for the City

In this prayer, the lines in italics are spoken by the People.

The Celebrant faces them and sings or says

The Lord be with you.
And also with you.

Lift up your hearts.
We lift them to the Lord.

Let us give thanks to God.
It is right to give our thanks and praise.

All praise to you, Eternal God, Architect of the Universe:
you laid the foundations of the earth with the rule of justice;
you set its cornerstone with the plumb line of righteousness
and gated the sea safely within its bounds.
With your Word and Wisdom you gave life to all creatures,
forming humanity in your image.
So with all creation, saints, and citizens of heaven, we sing (say):

Celebrant and People

Holy, holy, holy! God of power and might,
heaven and earth are full of your glory.
Hosanna in the highest.
Blessed is the one who comes in the name of the Lord.
Hosanna in the highest.

The Celebrant continues

From among the peoples of the world
you called Israel to be your Covenant People, your Redeemed,
led out of captivity to bear witness to your justice and love;
you established Jerusalem as a beacon,
a city to be Sought Out and Not Forsaken,
its trees with leaves for the healing of all nations.

But in every generation
those who would serve you turn aside instead in sin;
and we confess we have not preserved the welfare of the city
      where you have set us;
the earth lies polluted, the poor cry out in the streets,

oppression and fraud trouble the marketplaces;
our evil is in our homes and in our hearts,
and we have gone each one in our own way.

But you have never forsaken us in our sin;
you poured yourself out for us in love,
sending your only-begotten, Jesus, to be born of Mary
by your Holy Spirit's power.
Jesus traveled the cities and villages teaching,
healing the sick, proclaiming forgiveness
and the year of your favor, heaven come near.

On the night Jesus was handed over to suffering and death,
he gathered his friends at table.
Taking bread, he blessed and broke and gave it to them, saying:
"Take, eat. This is my Body given for you.
Do this for the remembrance of me."

After supper, he took a cup of wine,
gave thanks to you and gave it to his friends, saying:
"This cup is the new Covenant in my Blood,
shed for all for the forgiveness of sins;
whenever you drink it,
do this for the remembrance of me."

And so we offer you this bread and cup
and ourselves to be made living stones of your holy building,
a people renewed and consecrated to you.
Send your Spirit upon these gifts
that they may be the Body and Blood of Christ,
and upon us that we may serve you as your Body in the world
and always and everywhere acclaim:

Celebrant and People

Christ has died.
Christ is risen.
Christ will come again!

The Celebrant continues

Grant that we may build a city at unity with itself,
its streets safe to walk in, peace within its walls,
a river of living water flowing from its mercy-seat,
your Christ its Governor,
through, with, and in whom we give thanks and praise to you
in the Holy Spirit, now and for ever. *AMEN.*

Jennifer Phillips

NOTES

The line, "a city to be Sought Out and Not Forsaken," is taken from Isaiah 62:12.

The line, "its trees with leaves for the healing of all nations," comes from Revelation 22:2.

Transitions in the Life of a Congregation

Parish Welcome for the Newly Confirmed

—as the Church better understands the primacy of Holy Baptism within the life of a congregation, some episcopal authorities, in order to preserve and reaffirm that primacy, have removed the separate rite of Confirmation to the larger gathering of the diocese; this litany was written to welcome those confirmands into their parishes.

The Officiant asks the newly confirmed to come forward to be welcomed by the congregation.

The newly confirmed assemble and begin Psalm 84, with the congregation reading responsively.

1   How dear to me is your dwelling, O Lord of hosts!*
    My soul has a desire and longing for the courts of the Lord;
    my heart and my flesh rejoice in the living God.

2   *The sparrow has found her a house*
    and the swallow a nest where she may lay her young; *
    by the side of your altars, O Lord of hosts,
    my ruler and my God.

3   Happy are they who dwell in your house!*
    They will always be praising you.

4   *Happy are the people whose strength is in you,* *
    whose hearts are set on the pilgrims' way.

5   Those who go through the desolate valley will find
    it a place of springs*
    for the early rains have covered it with pools of water.

6   *They will climb from height to height,* *
    and the God of Gods will be revealed in Zion.

7   Lord God of hosts, hear my prayer;*
    listen, O God of Jacob.

8   *Behold our defender, O God:* *
    and look upon the face of your Anointed.

9 For one day in your courts is better than
   a thousand in my own room,*
    and to stand at the threshold of the house of my God
    than to dwell in the tents of the wicked.

10 *For the Lord is both sun and shield,* *
   and will give grace and glory;

11 No good thing will the Lord withhold*
   from those who walk with integrity.

12 *O Lord of hosts,* *
   Happy are they who put their trust in you!

Officiant

I charge you, the people of God at _____, to receive these newly confirmed members in Christ's name. Will you support them with your prayers, and hold them accountable for living adult lives in accordance with the Gospel and for taking their share in the mission, ministry, and council of the parish and the wider Church?

People We will!

Let us pray.

Come, Holy Spirit, Wind and Fire of Love:
so enliven the hearts and minds of these your servants,
N., N., and N., that they may be set ablaze with your
   love, impassioned for the work of justice,
persevering in seeking you,
generous in giving,
devoted in prayer,
and courageous in pouring out their lives
   to proclaim your good news to the world,
to your honor and glory. *Amen.*

Here, the names of the confirmed may be entered in the parish register in the sight of the people.

Jennifer Phillips

THANKSGIVING FOR THE RETURN TO CHURCH OF A SHUT-IN OR INFIRM MEMBER

O God of power and new life, you raised up by Jesus' hand the woman bent with infirmity that she might stand up and give you praise; we give you thanks for this *daughter* of Abraham, N., who has felt the strong grasp of your healing hand; grant that *she* may lift up *her* voice continually to you in gladness in the assembly of your people; through Jesus Christ our Savior. *Amen.*

Jennifer Phillips

FOR A MEMBER MOVING AWAY

O God, who led your chosen people as a pillar of fire by night and a pillar of cloud by day, go before N. [and N.] as *she continues her* Christian service in a new place and among a new community. Give *her* grace to show forth your love in all that *she does.* Receive our thanks for *her* life and ministry among us, and bless *her* on *her* way; through Jesus Christ our Savior. *Amen.*

Jennifer Phillips

THANKSGIVING FOR CAPITAL CAMPAIGN WORK

O merciful Creator, your hand is open wide to satisfy the needs of every living creature: we give you thanks for opening the hands and hearts of your people so that we may accomplish the work necessary to serve the Gospel. In particular, we give thanks for the completion of _____ as part of our capital campaign; and we acknowledge that all our abundance comes from you, and with it we are called to give you honor and glory; through Jesus Christ our Savior. *Amen.*

Jennifer Phillips

PASTORAL NEEDS

LITANY OF HEALING AND WHOLENESS

—based on the writings of Hildegard of Bingen

The Leader sings or says

God of all harmony: you are the music of life, the ground-note of our being. Hear us, for we have lost our bearings. Heal us for the sake of your Jesus. Fill our emptiness, and center our souls in you, we pray.

The Leader and People pray responsively

Inspire us with your holy Wisdom,
Strengthen our frailty.

Silence.

Send your Spirit to wash away our disease;
Release us from our brokenness.

Silence.

Anoint us where we are sick;
Give us your kiss of peace.

Silence.

Pour healing like the scent of balsam;
Make us clean and whole.

Silence.

Look on us lest we lose our hope;
Your power is our help in need.

Silence.

Calm the whirlwind of our unrest;
And bring us to the sunrise of your radiant life.

Silence.

Help us to become Christ's arms;
To comfort the world's misery.

Silence.

The Leader continues

God of love: bring us into your wholeness. Heal the sick for the sake of your Jesus. Fill our emptiness, and help us know the joy of your salvation. *Amen.*

Phoebe Pettingell

FOR SERENITY IN THE MIDST OF SUFFERING

—a prayer of private devotion

Glory to you, my Savior Jesus Christ, for your loving-kindness and fidelity in acceptance of fear and suffering for my salvation. In the strength of your grace, help me to bear my infirmities with hope and expectation, so that in union with your passion I may find peace in the power of your resurrection. Amen.

Gregory Howe

AFTER MISCARRIAGE OR STILLBIRTH

O God, Wellspring of all life and Giver of all good gifts, look kindly upon N. [and N.] who *has* conceived and lost a child. Hold *her* child, N., safely in your everlasting arms. Bring to *her* such comfort in loss that *she* may again rest all *her* hopes in you and rejoice in the blessing of your presence; in Christ's name we pray. *Amen.*

Jennifer Phillips

FOR THE LOSS OF A HOME TO FIRE

O God, repairer of the breach and comfort of the brokenhearted, rebuilder of the ruined places and replanter of that which was desolate, we pray for N. [and N.], who *have* lost a home to fire and who *mourn* its many memories. Help *them* to build up with patience and confidence, knowing that *their* true home is ever in you who make your home abiding with us your people. *Amen.*

Jennifer Phillips

FOR THE BEGINNING OF A NEW BUSINESS OR JOB

O God, who has begun a good work in us; we thank you for the courage and creativity of your servant N., who is beginning a new business [job]. Bring *her* labors to fruitfulness and grant that they may be for the building up of your reign in creation; and strengthen us all in the work to which you have called us in our covenant of baptism; through Jesus Christ our Savior. *Amen.*

Jennifer Phillips

For Discernment in a Relationship

Most Holy God, you bless us with loving hearts to nurture and care for one another; give to N. and N. wisdom to discern your will for their relationship, grace to see your face in one another, and steady affection to love and serve you in and beyond their relationship. May their lives and ours show forth your presence and glory; through Jesus Christ our Savior. *Amen.*

Jennifer Phillips

For the Coming Apart of a Close Relationship

O God of mercy and renewal, you look with compassion on all our frailties, sins, and broken hopes; hear our prayer for N. and N., in the coming apart of their relationship. Visit them with your strong presence for the healing of their hearts. Anchor each of them in the love and care of this community. Renew in them the wellsprings of life and joy, and grant that they may treat one another kindly and truthfully; and give to all of us who love them the grace and wisdom to uphold them in the time of trial; for your love's sake. *Amen.*

Jennifer Phillips

For Residences

Versicle The sparrow has found her a home and the swallow a nest where she may lay her young.

Response By the side of your altar, O Lord of hosts.

O God, in whom we find our true rest: we commend to your continual care the homes in which your people dwell. Let your holy angels dwell with them to preserve them in peace, and let your blessing be upon them always; through Jesus Christ our Savior. *Amen.*

Jennifer Phillips

FOR FATHERS

Gracious God, our heavenly Father, from whom all fatherhood is modeled and by whom every family in heaven and earth is named; we thank you for our fathers: for those who have come to you, we pray your grace and mercy, for those who are still with us, we pray the courage and wisdom of Joseph, whom you gave to be the guardian of our Savior Jesus Christ. *Amen.*

Gregory Howe

FOR MOTHERS

Gracious and everliving God, you called a brave young woman to be the mother of your Son. We thank you for the courage, love, and nurture of our mothers; for the living, grant them the honor they deserve; for the departed, your grace and mercy, for the sake of our Savior Jesus Christ. *Amen.*

Gregory Howe

PASTORAL OFFICES

FOR THE LIGHTING OF WEDDING CANDLES FROM THE PASCHAL CANDLE

—written especially for use in marriage ceremonies
without Eucharist or a ring ceremony.

Instead of a ring ceremony, or following directly after, wedding candles are lighted by the couple from the Paschal Candle to symbolize the light of Christ coming into their home and marriage.

The Presider sings or says

O God, our Light and Wisdom,
as the Paschal Candle reminds us of that holy night of Easter
in which earth and heaven are joined
and we are reconciled to God,
may these candles be a sign of the reconciling love
by which you join the lives of these two people
in your one everlasting Light. *Amen.*

Jennifer Phillips

IN A TIME OF BEREAVEMENT

O gracious Savior, God's Word spoken to us for life; look with compassion upon N. [and N.], whose *heart is* bowed down with grief for N., who has died. Comfort *her* as you comforted Mary in the garden that *she* may recognize your resurrection presence, and help us all to know that as we dwell in the shadow of death, your angel has already rolled away the stone to summon us into eternal life, where you live and reign with the Author and Spirit of life; one God for ever and ever. *Amen.*

Jennifer Phillips

PRAYER FOR A REQUIEM EUCHARIST

In the presence of the One who will call us from our graves, cleansed in the blood of the Lamb, consoled by the Holy Spirit and in union with the saints of every time and place, let us offer our prayers to the God who loves us, saying, "Hear and have mercy."

For the holy Church of God, that Christ our Savior may confirm it in faith, sustain it in hope, and anchor its union in love, let us pray to the God who loves us.
Hear and have mercy.

For those entrusted with earthly power, that they may do justice, love mercy, and walk humbly before the true ruler of the universe; so that all the peoples of the earth may rejoice in your goodness; let us pray to the God who loves us.
Hear and have mercy.

For this assembly, gathered to make Eucharist in communion with the Church in this world and the next, that formed by our baptism, nourished by the word of truth and the bread of life, we may live and witness the gospel of Christ, let us pray to the God who loves us.
Hear and have mercy.

For those who mourn [especially N. and N.], that casting all their sorrow and pain at the foot of the cross, they may know the consolation of your love, let us pray to the God who loves us.
Hear and have mercy.

For all who are bereaved, that by the love and care of Jesus' blessed mother, they may find strength to meet the days ahead in the comfort of a holy and certain hope, and in the joyful expectation of reunion with those they love, let us pray to the God who loves us.
Hear and have mercy.

Finally, for those who have departed this life in faith, especially N. As we entrust *her* to your never-failing love and mercy, which sustained *her* in this life, we ask you to receive *her* as your own, according to the favor you have shown to your people. Let us pray to the God who loves us.
Hear and have mercy.

God of all consolation, as Jesus wept for his friend, extend compassion and grace to your people in their sorrow. Be our refuge and our strength, to lift us from the night of our grief to the peace and light of your presence; through Jesus Christ our Redeemer, who died that we might live. *Amen.*

Gregory Howe

OTHER PRAYERS

PRAYERS OF THE PEOPLE

—this prayer and the eucharistic prayer which follows were written for a celebration of the Diocese of Delaware, honoring its companion relationship with the Diocese of Pretoria, South Africa.

Leader

In peace and in faith, let us offer our prayers, saying, "Christ, have mercy."

For peace, justice, and equity in the world, and for the salvation of all, let us pray.

Here and after every petition the People respond

Christ, have mercy.

For all who confess the name of Christ, that they may be filled with the power of the Holy Spirit, let us pray.
Christ, have mercy.

For N., our Presiding Bishop, N., our Bishop, and for all the holy people of God, that they may be faithful to their calling, let us pray.
Christ, have mercy.

For N., our President, for the leaders of the nations, and for all in authority, that your people may live in peace and security, let us pray.
Christ, have mercy.

For all peoples, that they may know the glory you have given in the unity and diversity of the human family, let us pray.
Christ, have mercy.

For the victims of injustice, violence, and hatred, and those who minister to them, that you will be their help and defense, let us pray.
Christ, have mercy.

For ourselves, that our hearts may be cleansed from prejudice and selfishness; that by your grace we may hunger and thirst for what is right, let us pray.
Christ, have mercy.

For those who are sick in body or in mind [especially *N.* and *N.*], that *they* may be made whole by your grace, let us pray.
Christ, have mercy.

For those who are bound by fear and despair, that they may be delivered to the liberty of your children, let us pray.
Christ, have mercy.

For those condemned to exile, unjust imprisonment, or hazardous labor for the sake of justice and truth, that you will support them in their witness, let us pray.
Christ, have mercy.

For the faithful departed [especially *N.* and *N.*]; for a peaceful end and eternal rest to all who are dying, and your comfort for all who mourn, let us pray.
Christ, have mercy.

Gregory Howe

EUCHARISTIC PRAYER

—this eucharistic prayer and the prayers of the people preceding it were written for a celebration of the Diocese of Delaware, honoring its companion relationship with the Diocese of Pretoria, South Africa.

In this prayer, the lines in italics are spoken by the People.

The Celebrant faces them and sings or says

The Lord be with you.
And also with you.

Lift up your hearts.
We lift them to the Lord.

Let us give thanks to the Lord our God.
It is right to give God thanks and praise.

Gracious God, we give you thanks and praise for the gift of a world full of wonder, and for our life which comes from you. By your power you sustain the universe.
Glory to God for ever and ever.

You created us to love you with all our heart, and to love each other as ourselves, but we have rejected the wonder of the diversity of races and cultures which you gave us so that we might know you in all your majesty, and we rebel against you by the evil that we do.

In Jesus, you brought healing to our world and gathered us into one great family. Through the powerful and graceful witness of your saints, you have enriched our vision of the people called together by your love in the redeeming power of our Savior.
Glory to God for ever and ever.

And so we join the saints and angels in proclaiming your glory as we sing (say):

Celebrant and People

Holy, holy, holy Lord, God of power and might,
heaven and earth are full of your glory.
Hosanna in the highest.
Blessed is the one who comes in the name of the Lord.
Hosanna in the highest.

The Celebrant continues

Holy and everliving God, we bless your name, because, in sending Jesus, you showed how much you love us. Caring for the poor and the hungry, Jesus nurtured the sick and rejected.

Betrayed and forsaken, our Savior did not despair, but overcame hatred with love. On the cross he defeated the power of sin and death. By raising Jesus from the dead, you show us the power of your love to bring new life to all your people.
Glory to God for ever and ever.

On the night before he died for us, our Savior Jesus Christ took bread, and giving thanks to you, he broke it, gave it to the disciples, and said: "Take, eat: This is my Body which is given for you. Do this for the remembrance of me."

As supper was ending, Jesus took the cup of wine, and having given thanks to you, he gave it to them saying: "Drink this, all of you: This is my Blood of the new Covenant, which is poured out for you and for all for the forgiveness of sins. Whenever you drink it, do this for the remembrance of me."

In faith we acclaim you, O Christ:

Celebrant and People

Dying, you destroyed our death.
Rising, you restored our life.
Christ Jesus, come in glory.

The Celebrant continues

Remembering now the suffering and death and proclaiming the resurrection and ascension of Jesus our Redeemer, we bring before you these gifts. Sanctify them by your Holy Spirit to be for your people the Body and Blood of Christ. We ask you to send your Holy Spirit upon this, your gathered Church: fill us with your Holy Spirit, and confirm our faith in your truth; that together we may praise you and give you glory; through our Savior Jesus Christ.
Glory to God for ever and ever.

Through Christ and with Christ and in Christ, in the unity of the Holy Spirit, to you be honor, glory, and praise, for ever and ever. AMEN.

Gregory Howe

A LITANY OF REMEMBRANCE

—this litany and the eucharistic prayer which follows were written for the tenth-anniversary celebration of the Council for Women's Ministries of the Episcopal Church.

Let us remember and give thanks for faithful women of God, that their lives may inspire ours.
For Miriam, prophet who led the women of Israel in rejoicing at their deliverance from Egypt;
For the unnamed woman who acted as prophet and anointed Jesus before his burial;
God of abundant life,
We give you thanks.

That we may claim our gifts of leadership and have courage to announce your truth by our words and actions;
God of graceful power,
We offer our prayer.

For Joanna and Susanna, disciples who followed Jesus and supported him in his ministry;
For Mary Magdalene, disciple and first witness to the resurrection, who proclaimed the Good News;
For women leaders in the early Church: for Phoebe, Prisca, and Junia;
God of abundant life,
We give you thanks.

That we and all your Church may follow Christ faithfully and bear witness to the good news of God in Christ Jesus;
God of graceful power,
We offer our prayer.

For the woman who had hemorrhaged for twelve years, and dared to touch the hem of your garment;
For the woman who had been bent over for eighteen years and came to you for healing;
God of abundant life,
We give you thanks.

That we may recognize your healing grace and be healed from all that weakens or cripples us;
That your healing grace may be with any who are sick or suffering;
God of graceful power,
We offer our prayer.

For women mystics of the Middle Ages: for Hildegard of Bingen, Teresa of Ávila, and Julian of Norwich, who used many names and images to praise you and tell of your goodness and love;
God of abundant life,
We give you thanks.

That we may know you ever more deeply and praise you as one God with many names;
God of graceful power,
We offer our prayer.

For the women of this country who fought against slavery and worked for justice for all people: for Sojourner Truth, Harriet Ross Tubman, Eleanor Roosevelt, Rosa Parks;
For the women who struggled for women's rights: for Elizabeth Cady Stanton and Susan B. Anthony;
God of abundant life,
We give you thanks.

That we may be empowered to strive for justice and peace among all people;
God of graceful power,
We offer our prayer.

For women of the Episcopal Church who were leaders in mission and ministry: for Mary Abbott Emery Twing, first national secretary of the Women's Auxiliary; for Julia Chester Emery, leader of the Women's Auxiliary for forty years; for Susan Knapp, deaconess and Dean of the New York Training School for Deaconesses;
For the work of the Council for Women's Ministries, as we celebrate our tenth year, and for the member organizations of the Council;
God of abundant life,
We give you thanks.

That we may be faithful to the ministries to which you call us;
God of graceful power,
We offer our prayer.

Life-giving God, you have healed and empowered women throughout all ages,
Grant that we may follow their examples and live faithfully as your people in the world, in the name of Jesus Christ. Amen.
Ruth A. Meyers

EUCHARISTIC PRAYER

—this eucharistic prayer and the litany preceding it were written
for the tenth-anniversary celebration of the
Council for Women's Ministries of the Episcopal Church

In this prayer, the lines in italics are spoken by the People.

The Celebrant faces them and sings or says

The Lord be with you.
And also with you.

Lift up your hearts.
We lift them to the Lord.

Let us give thanks to the Lord our God.
It is right to give God thanks and praise.

We praise you and we thank you, strong and faithful God,
wellspring of life and womb of mercy.
Through your Word you brought all things into being;
Through your Wisdom you formed us in your image, female and male.

You called Israel into covenant with you.
You delivered your people from slavery in Egypt,
and led them in safety through the Red Sea.
In the cry of the prophets,
you called for justice and offered hope for salvation.

And so we join the saints and angels in proclaiming your glory,
as we sing (say):

Celebrant and People

Holy, holy, holy Lord, God of power and might,
heaven and earth are full of your glory.
Hosanna in the highest.
Blessed is the one who comes in the name of the Lord.
Hosanna in the highest.

The Celebrant continues

Holy indeed are you, O God, and blessed is your servant Jesus,
who became flesh in the womb of Mary,
that we might know your wisdom and your love,
and be led from slavery into freedom, from death into new life.

Blessed is your servant Jesus,
who proclaimed release to the captives,
who broke bread with Mary and Martha,
who welcomed and blessed the little children.
Blessed is your servant Jesus,
who, before he suffered,
yearned to eat the Passover of liberation with his companions.
On the night before he died for us,
our Savior Jesus Christ took bread,
and when he had given thanks to you,
he broke it, and gave it to his friends, and said:
"Take, eat: This is my Body, which is given for you.
Do this for the remembrance of me."

As supper was ending, Jesus took the cup of wine,
and when he had given thanks, he gave it to them, and said:
"Drink this, all of you:
This is my Blood of the new Covenant,
which is poured out for you and for all
for the forgiveness of sins.
Whenever you drink it, do this for the remembrance of me."

In faith we acclaim you, O Christ:

Celebrant and People

Dying, you restored our death.
Rising, you restored our life.
Christ Jesus, come in glory.

The Celebrant continues

Remembering now the suffering and death
and proclaiming the resurrection and ascension
of Jesus our Redeemer,
we bring before you these gifts.
Sanctify them by your Holy Spirit
to be for your people the Body and Blood of Christ.
Pour out your Holy Spirit upon us,
that we may be the Body of Christ,
offered in love for the world you have made.

Remember the faithful service of holy women throughout the ages.
Remember those who have touched our lives
and led us more deeply into discipleship,
especially those we now name before you:

The People may add names of those significant to them.

The Celebrant continues

Remember all who have died in the peace of Christ,
and those whose faith is known to you alone;
bring them into the place of eternal joy and light.
Grant that in the fullness of time we may join with all your saints
to sing your praises and feast at your heavenly banquet.

Through Christ and with Christ and in Christ,
in the unity of the Holy Spirit,
to you be honor, glory, and praise, for ever and ever. *AMEN.*

Ruth A. Meyers

COMFORTABLE WORDS

—adapted from Matthew 11:28–30

Come to Jesus, all whose life is hard, whose load is heavy; and find assured relief. Accept Jesus' yoke and learn from your Savior, for your redeemer is gentle and humble and your souls will find peace; for that yoke is good to bear and your God will lighten your load.

Gregory Howe

PRAYER AND PRAISE

Gracious and everliving God, as we come to bless your holy name in prayer and praise, send us your Holy Spirit, that, fired by your grace, we may rejoice in the presence of our Savior and be bearers of Christ to our friends and neighbors. *Amen.*

Gregory Howe

PRAYERS FROM THE MOTHERS
OF THE CHURCH

A PRAYER OF MERCY AND JUSTICE

—after Hildegard of Bingen

Gracious God, fill us with your wisdom,
and in your mercy guide us
along the paths of justice. *Amen.*

Phoebe Pettingell

A PRAYER TO THE TRINITY

—after Julian of Norwich

Trinity of Truth—our Father: you made us and preserve us.
Trinity of Wisdom—our Mother: you comfort us in love.
Trinity of Goodness—our God: fill us with your grace.

Phoebe Pettingell

A PRAYER FOR THE COMING OF THE COMFORTER

—after Catherine of Siena

Loving God: send your Holy Spirit, your Comforter, into our hearts. Bring us home by your power, that we may love you. Let every burden seem light in the face of your love. *Amen.*

Phoebe Pettingell